BEYOND BUZZ

BEYOND BUZZ

The Next Generation
of Word-of-Mouth Marketing

LOIS KELLY

AMACOM

American Management Association

New York • Atlanta • Brussels • Chicago • Mexico City
San Francisco • Shanghai • Tokyo • Toronto • Washington, D.C.

Special discounts on bulk quantities of AMACOM books are available to corporations, professional associations, and other organizations. For details, contact Special Sales Department, AMACOM, a division of American Management Association, 1601 Broadway, New York, NY 10019.
Tel.: 212-903-8316. Fax: 212-903-8083.
E-mail: specialsls@amanet.org
Web site: www.amacombooks.org/go/specialsales
To view all AMACOM titles go to: www.amacombooks.org

This publication is designed to provide accurate and authoritative information in regard to the subject matter covered. It is sold with the understanding that the publisher is not engaged in rendering legal, accounting, or other professional service. If legal advice or other expert assistance is required, the services of a competent professional person should be sought.

Various names used by companies to distinguish their software and other products can be claimed as trademarks. AMACOM uses such names throughout this book for editorial purposes only, with no intention of trademark violation. All such software or product names are in initial capital letters or ALL CAPITAL letters. Individual companies should be contacted for complete information regarding trademarks and registration.

Library of Congress Cataloging-in-Publication Data

Kelly, Lois 1955-
    Beyond buzz : the next generation of word-of-mouth marketing / Lois Kelly.
        p.   cm.
    Includes index.
    ISBN-10: 0-8144-7383-0 (hardcover)
    ISBN-13: 978-0-8144-7383-2 (hardcover)
    1. Communication in marketing.   2. Marketing.   I. Title.
HF5415.123.K45   2007
658.8—dc22

                                        2006036160

Printed in the United States of America.

Printing number

10   9   8   7   6   5   4   3   2   1

"The newest computer can merely compound, at speed, the oldest problem in the relations between human beings, and in the end the communicator will be confronted with the old problem, of what to say and how to say it."

—Edward R. Murrow

Contents

- Being relevant: Beyond acts of God and Congress
- Love this: Emotion is the superhighway to meaning
- Meaning-making lessons for the five-year-old mind in all of us

x • Contents

BEYOND BUZZ

New marketing is about conversations—listening, having something new to add, and talking like we mean it instead of hiding behind prepackaged corporate-speak.

It's about being more interested in the world outside our companies than the world inside our companies and sharing ideas that go beyond the company and its products. It's about things that help people get to know us in ways that build understanding, trust, and feelings that make them want to do business with our companies.

Back in the late 1990s *The Cluetrain Manifesto* authors sounded the alarm for this shift to marketing conversations. Popular marketing author Seth Godin has continued the call for new ways to connect with customers. And executives such as Procter & Gamble's global marketing officer, Jim Stengel, have been speaking out on the need to more meaningfully engage with customers because the old marketing model is dead. The boom in new conversational tactics like blogs and online communities underscores how much people want to talk about ideas and opinions in a human voice, not just be *talked to* about products and promotions.

"You mean to say so much of what we've been doing all these years needs to change? The messaging, the media training, the advertising, even the writing style?" asked a marketing executive after hearing one of my speeches.

Before I could reply, she said, "You don't have to tell me. I know. I know. I know. We absolutely have to change. It's not about our company or our products. It's about what people want to know and talking with them in the ways they want. How we want to do things doesn't matter. We're not in control."

Marketing's purpose is to involve customers, helping them to understand the value of an organization or product to their wants and needs. The metaphor for marketing is no longer an advertising and brochure manufacturing plant. It is more like a blue ribbon school. Like great teaching, the goal of marketing is not to assert conclusions but to engage an audience in a dialogue, which leads people to discoveries of their own.

My intent in writing this book is to share with you some ways that can help make a big difference to your organization's marketing success and to your career. I've included the templates, frameworks, questions, and shortcuts I use in my consulting firm. I've applied these principles to multibillion-dollar corporations and to start-ups, to business-to-business organizations and to consumer products companies.

Change is hard, as is letting go of marketing message control. But conversational marketing is easier than the old ways. There are more ways to listen to what customers are interested in and want to talk about. The guesswork about the right messages is gone. If we listen, customers will tell us what they want to know and learn.

Searching for the so-called big creative idea isn't necessary.

We don't need expensive copywriters, a specially crafted brand voice, and big campaigns to reach customers. We just have to talk with people in our own style, through direct channels—from conference calls and small salonlike conferences to blogs and online communities.

If it's not a conversation, then it's not effective marketing. This book will show you how to succeed in this new conversational marketing world.

Moving into the talk world: Ten introductory thoughts

1. Have a point of view (or several)
2. Talk like you talk
3. Listen more
4. Give more advice
5. Invite more people in, get out more
6. Tap into what's bubbling
7. Make people feel heard
8. Talk like you mean it
9. Ask more questions
10. Be brave

Chapter 1

Enough with the marketing blah blah blah— let's talk about something interesting

The conversations in marketing circles say it's time for a revolution, and most of the talk is around new tactics. You might hear them say:

* "The old marketing rules are dead."
* "TV commercials don't work. Advertising agencies are dinosaurs."
* "Your CEO needs to blog. Or do monthly Podcasts."
* "Word-of-mouth marketing is the Next Big Thing."
* "Public relations is more important than advertising."
* "Get ready for advertising on video iPods!"
* "It's time to break down the marketing silos."

The big new idea isn't about new tactics, although they're certainly exciting and opening up new communications channels. The big idea is simply that marketing is about having conversations and engaging with people in interesting discussions, through new and traditional channels. Technology may be becoming the heart of marketing and communications, but conversations are the soul.

John Battelle, a founder of *Wired* and *The Industry Standard*, recently said, "Marketing has become a science on one hand and conversation on the other. In other words, we need to have a real conversation to get down to the thing we're supposed to be good at: communication. Not selling, not grabbing attention, not seducing. Communicating. It sounds obvious, but in fact it requires an entirely new approach to marketing."[1]

This book shows you how to evolve your practices to succeed in a marketing-conversation world. It's a marketing field guide of sorts. In it, you'll discover:

* What conversational marketing is and why it has become an important addition to the marketing mix
* How to find ideas and points of view that help people talk about your company in ways that are interesting to customers and develop mutual understanding
* How to evolve traditional marketing practices into more of a two-way dialogue
* How to overcome the obstacles to conversational marketing and change your organization

People should like talking about your company

What do people in your company talk about to people outside the company? Do people like telling your story? Do the conversations add up—or are they random talk? Do they help explain what makes your company different? Get people interested enough so that they put aside competitors to learn more about you? Jump-start meaningful conversations so that sales cycles move faster? Build trust? Make people feel good about buying from you?

Conversations should do these things, but many don't. So customers, analysts, or reporters often walk away from a meeting unclear or unable to talk about what was especially interesting or relevant.

This is because no one in marketing, sales, or communications is yet responsible for conversations. (Chapter 8 provides ideas for new roles and responsibilities.) Traditional marketing and communications don't help people talk. Advertising and direct marketing promote. Web sites and public relations inform. Vision, mission, and values statements are directional. Messaging documents are too often written to be read, not said. And the ubiquitous elevator speeches are usually starched, self-absorbed, and, well, descriptive. They don't help jump-start a conversation that gets people to say, "Gee that's interesting. Tell me more." They might tell, but they don't engage. See Figure 1-1 for a snapshot

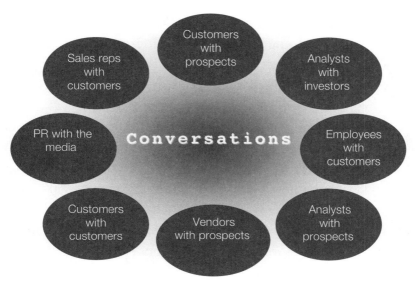

Figure 1-1. Common conversations that influence sales decisions.

of all the possible conversations that can take place in organizations.

Want the sales reps to make more calls? Give them something interesting to talk about.

Want frontline supervisors to be better communicators with employees? Give them something interesting to talk about.

Wish the CEO were a more engaging speaker? Give her something interesting to talk about.

Want the PR people to get more media stories? Give them something editors will find interesting.

Lights out in San Francisco: Lessons from a blackout

A few years ago I was in a San Francisco hotel conference room with a smart, witty marketing vice president of a software company called Firepond. We were waiting for a group of international business journalists to arrive for a ten o'clock meeting where Steve was going to introduce the journalists to the company and its products.

Steve was especially nervous because the CEO usually did these types of meetings and the company's software was complex. He ran through his PowerPoint slides three times to make sure he was set, making some minor tweaks here and there. He was feeling especially good about several new slides that showed how the different software modules fit together and how they connected to other technologies. It had taken months to figure out how to present the software system visually, and Steve was confident the journalists could now understand the software when they saw these slides.

Just as we were about to get the presentation under way, the electricity went down. The entire city of San Francisco was without power. Steve, usually a pretty cool guy, was stunned, stuttering and at a loss. No PowerPoint? How could he explain the company? You couldn't understand the software if you couldn't see the slides.

The journalists were quite kind, suggesting that Steve forget about "presenting" and just talk with them. Tell some customer stories. Explain how the company was different from the big competitors. Better yet, they wanted to know why a well-known German software executive—the CEO—had decided to go to a small software company like Firepond?

Steve spent most of the time talking about the German CEO. He explained that the CEO had been extremely frustrated when he ran large sales organizations at other companies and didn't think that any of the existing sales automation or customer relationship management software actually helped the sales rep.

Steve then tried to draw on the whiteboard how the software worked. But with no air-conditioning the room was growing hotter and the journalists' interest was cooling. The power came back and everyone cheered and we all decided to leave the building while the elevator worked. No time was left to see how those software modules worked.

On their way out, several journalists said, in effect, "We like the story about why your CEO left his big job at SAP to start this company. Could you set up a time for us to talk to him—and maybe a couple of your customers? We think that would be more interesting to our European audiences than the technical product information."

In that dark, hot conference room I realized that despite all the strategy, positioning, and messaging advice I had provided to Steve, I had failed. What Steve needed—and, I'm sure, many, many others—was ideas on how to have interesting and memorable conversations that engage an audience and help them understand what was different and valuable about the company.

My epiphany was confirmed when, as we were shaking hands good-bye, one editor whispered to me, "All these software products . . . it's too much even for us Germans. I really don't care so much how they work."

Eventually, Firepond did get comfortable talking in new ways, and Steve became much more comfortable talking than presenting. The point of view that eventually helped Steve and the rest of the sales team talk about Firepond software was that "sales reps don't want typical sales automation software for writing reports back at the Holiday Inn. They want a way to give prospects customized product recommendations on the spot, no matter how complex the product. That's what we do, sales recommendation software for when you're *with* a prospect."[2]

> ## To provoke conversations, have something interesting to talk about

Countless sales reps, public relations managers, and CEOs struggle like Steve and I did during that power failure to figure out how to do a better job engaging prospects, media, and employees. Too often, our instinct is to create new tactics without considering how to improve the conversation. Or we heap on more rational facts and figures to support our point, like a lawyer preparing a brief. Yet, facts alone don't necessarily help people understand what we're talking about—or even make them want to have conversations with us.

We need interesting ideas that both provoke conversations and involve people in the conversations. Studies have found that the more customers participate in meaningful conversations and interactions with companies, the more likely they are to purchase a product or service and recommend it to others.[3] For marketers, this suggests that we need to find ways to involve customers in more conversations that are meaningful to them.

One step is to create conversational marketing approaches, such as salonlike meetings, online customer communities, more regular radio talk show–like conference calls, and more conversational sales meetings. The second step is having something interesting to talk about in those conversations. Some of the most effective conversation starters are points of view based on beliefs, contrarian views, or unusual advice. A good point of view gently (or not so gently) smacks people in the face and gets the response, "That's interesting. Tell me more." It lures people into the conversation, sparking dialogue that helps us understand issues, products, and companies in multidimensional, rational, and emotional ways.

Marketing as a good dinner party conversationalist[4]

If the metaphor for marketing is a conversation, then marketing should be like a good dinner party host who:

❑ Has a fresh point of view, but never tries to thrust it on other guests
❑ Speaks politely and respectfully
❑ Tells good stories to illustrate key points
❑ Is good at drawing other people's views out and drawing them into the conversation
❑ Speaks intelligently on a variety of subjects but is not afraid to admit areas of ignorance
❑ Avoids trotting out well-worn arguments that have been made time and time again
❑ Listens with genuine interest
❑ Is light-hearted in style, but always respectful of the other guests' points of view

People always ask, "Does a conversation theme replace something we already do like value propositions and product messaging?" The answer is no. Conversation themes are important *additions* to the traditional marketing tool kit.

Obstacles to conversational marketing

A second frequent question is, "If creating conversational marketing is as effective as you say, why aren't more companies doing it?" They aren't because of the following reasons:

• *No one is in charge* of conversational marketing from a strategic point of view. Individual functions may look at how to use new tactics to make programs more interesting and interactive, but few organizations have begun to think of marketing as conversations and to create the approaches and competencies needed to support that strategy.

• *"Alpha fraidy cats" are trying to take everyone's suggestions* into account. Often, when this happens, the committee produces a meaningless message mush. When a true point of view is put on the whiteboard, an alpha fraidy cat convinces everyone, "We can't say that," or "It doesn't explain enough of our story," or "Some prospects might not like us talking about that." (Alpha fraidy cats are persuasive, smart, articulate, domineering, often charming, and command respect because of their overt self-confidence. But underneath that smooth veneer, alpha fraidy cats are risk averse and self-doubting, particularly of people in their own organization; they think outsiders are smarter. They also instinctively pick apart why an idea won't work before allowing the idea time to breathe.)

• *Executives are suffering from executive attention disorder (EAD).* EAD executives quickly tire of talking about the same thing and always seem to want to talk about something new, usually before any one idea or view becomes known or understood.

• *Someone forgets to involve communications professionals* who have greater insights into what makes for genuine, interesting conversations. Often, they'll know more than marketing executives who were trained in traditional "telling" techniques like advertising, direct mail, and promotions.

• *The strategy is muddled.* The last obstacle is tricky. If there is no clear business strategy or a company is run by insecure executives (or both), it may be difficult to develop and get buy-in to conversation themes, which by their nature stir up interest, discussion, and questions.

When Eric Schmidt was CEO of the billion-dollar technology company Novell, sales reps, analysts, and journalists couldn't understand his strategy. He spoke often, but to increasingly confused people. No one could really figure out Novell's value to customers, including the sales reps and the customers themselves.

"Eric Schmidt is one of the great technologists of our time. But when it comes to marketing, he's been as clear as a foggy night in London, which has put Novell in a pickle," wrote David Einstein of *Forbes*. "It seems the salespeople at Novell have had a hard time conveying Schmidt's message." [5]

While Schmidt grappled to explain the strategy of being a Net services and software provider and sales reps tried to figure out what they were supposed to be selling, Novell's financial results plummeted. The once profitable company slid into years of quarter-million-dollar losses, suggesting that the problem may not have been just one of communications.

Too much jargon often signals bigger underlying business problems.

Why conversational marketing matters

Why are conversations—and having something interesting to talk about—important? The following three trends have turned traditional marketing and communications norms on their heads:

1. Less consumer trust in companies
2. Technology
3. The struggle to make sense out of so many choices and so much available information

People are listening to and talking with one another—and with those they view as trustworthy, credible, and having something interesting to say. For the most part, this does not include companies. Surveys say that people don't trust companies and that the only way to win back that trust is through communicating in new ways. Approximately 69 percent of Americans say "I just don't know whom to trust anymore," reports a Golin/Harris trust survey.[6] Two-thirds to four-fifths of Americans "display a profound distrust" of corporations, according to a Yankelovich "State of Consumer Trust" study.[7]

Customers want straightforward communications that address their interests.

"The inept marketers are the ones who fold their arms and

insist that you listen to their story and tell your story the way they want it told," says marketing author Seth Godin. "But the people aren't listening."[8]

Approximately 65 percent of respondents to the Golin/Harris trust study said that companies should do a better job understanding *their* needs and 93 percent said that companies should "communicate more clearly, effectively, and straightforwardly" to win back their trust. As former governor Gary Hart said in a *Washington Post* editorial that provoked nationwide political conversations, "The public trust must be earned and speaking clearly, candidly, and forcefully [about the mess in Iraq] is the place to begin."[9]

The second shift is that technology has made it possible to talk *with* people in many ways—from inexpensive global conference calls to informal blogs, where everyone has a chance to talk back to the speaker or writer. We're talking with people constantly—even if the "talk" is in written forms like online communities, instant messages, or e-mail.

These new channels have not only changed where we communicate, but how we communicate. Today communicating is direct and informal. Just as business dress has turned casual in all but a handful of major urban areas, so has business communications. We often tune out the overly formal in favor of people who are more direct and plainspoken.

Recently, I was researching companies that are doing interesting work in business innovation. I checked out two competitive companies: IBM and Sapient. On IBM's Web site I found an interview transcript of a conversation with Michael Zisman, vice president of corporate strategy. The interviewer asked Zisman, "How can companies begin the shift from productivity to innovation?" Zisman answered:

You have to understand that in a context of what companies face today, which is (A) a recognition that we're coming out of a recession, (B) that we are moving towards a global economy. So we're surrounded by change everywhere. And firms today are asking the question, "What is the evolving ecosystem in which I exist? How is the value chain disaggregating, unbundling, whatever term you want to use, but being broken up into pieces? What role do we want to play? Where do we have differentiating capabilities in that value chain where we can focus to really add value?"[10]

Say what? I'm sure IBM has some significant expertise in innovation, but I couldn't tell you what it is from this conversation with Zisman.

When I met with Stuart Moore, the cofounder of Sapient, a business and IT consulting firm, and asked the same question, he said, "There's no mystery to innovation. You just have to look through a new lens to see the possibilities. In many ways innovation is free."

The possibilities are everywhere and may even be free? That's interesting. Tell me more.

When I reported back to my colleagues, I recommended that we look more closely at Sapient because of the conversation with Moore. I was concerned that IBM might not have a strong strategy because Zisman used so much rhetoric. And, I admit, I thought it would be more interesting to talk with Moore. He seemed smart, yet pragmatic. A rational reason? No, but as you'll read in Chapter 2, when we're trying to understand new ideas, emotion and feelings play a big role in our decisions.

(As an aside: Months later, another IBM executive provided a different point of view on innovation that got me to say, "That's interesting. I'd like to hear more," which is the mark of a good point of view. "If you're not fast, you're dead. But if you're not also good, you're still dead," said George Bailey, a consultant at IBM's Business Consulting Group to a *Business Week* reporter.[11])

The third reason for conversational marketing is that we want to talk with people to understand choices and the people and companies behind the products. Unlike buzz marketing, which is someone recommending a good product or reviewing a disappointing experience, conversational marketing helps people make sense of ideas through two-way dialogues. Talking with people is how most of us learn, make sense of information, form relationships, and make decisions. It's part of our human nature, especially around new or complex ideas. The more complex or high-risk a decision, the more we value conversations to help understand the people, the product or service, the company, and other relevant factors.

This "sense making" is rooted in the educational psychology principle of "meaning making." Neurologists and educational psychologists have found that relevance, context, pattern making, and emotion are the four ingredients needed to get people to pay attention, understand what is being said, and then process and remember it. All conversations that help "make meaning" must have at least one of these ingredients, which Chapter 2 explains in detail.

Interestingly, emotion is the most powerful ingredient for understanding.

Yet, much marketing, sales, and corporate communications are sterile. There is no passion or conviction or even an occasional outrage. People are regularly numbed by PowerPoint presentations at meetings in dim rooms. They're lulled into daydreaming while listening to someone read a script during a teleconference. And they're suspect of corporate spokespersons who hide their personalities and passion behind scripted, re-hearsed responses.

This is too bad, because emotion not only drives good communications but influences whether a person will act based on a conversation.

> ## Three steps for real, relevant, and repeatable conversations

Here are three steps to creating interesting, relevant conversations.

1. Research in new ways, listening more closely and seeing new patterns

One of the fastest ways to create points of view that engage people is to tune in to what people are talking about and how they're talking with one another. Although typical market research might be just the thing for product management or geographic expansion planning, it often doesn't provide enough of the right kinds of insights for meaningful communication. Here are several approaches, all of which are explained more thoroughly in Chapter 4.

* *Tap into CEO beliefs.* CEOs and other C-level executives are attuned to emerging conversations because they're talking to more people in the market than anyone else in the company except, perhaps, for sales. What are the CEOs' views on customer frustrations, reasons for not making decisions, or uncertainties about the company?

* *Do a structured listening tour.* Get inside the heads of customers, noncustomers, industry experts, industry watchers, and

your own best sales reps. Talk with them individually about what is most relevant in their worlds, what is moving them to try new things—and what they couldn't care less about. What ideas and trends are they beginning to keep an eye on? What are the one or two obstacles that are annoying them to no end?

• *"See" what is being talked about.* Use new technology tools that visually show conversation topic patterns in any industry. Being able to see what the most popular topics are—and who and what is linked to them—is a way to glean ideas about which conversation themes may be most relevant to customers. The tools also help people understand the context within which these themes, or topics, are being discussed.

2. Create conversation themes based on points of view
Two things make a point of view stand out:

* It provokes conversation—be it contrarian, surprising, or challenging.
* It is something someone might actually say.

A point of view is not meant to be the headline of a Web site or the tag line on business cards. It's not meant to explain the company's entire value proposition. It is meant to get people thinking and talking. Here's an example.

When working with Hyperion, a large business analytics firm, I found that the team of marketing and communications people all instinctively liked the concept of talking about Hyperion as the company for chief operating officers (COOs).

At the time, competitors were targeting IT and e-business managers and they were talking deep technology talk. Hyperion provided a view into all of a company's operations, helping execs to see what was going on, make decisions, and hold people accountable. Unlike its competitors, it really could say it was the firm for COOs—and there was a lot of contrarian advice coming from COOs who early on had had it up to here with e-mania.

Taking a contrarian and counterintuitive approach to the market talk would have helped Hyperion to be noticed more quickly. It would have set the company apart, giving sales reps, partners, analysts, and the PR staff something to talk about. Plus, the CEO Jeff Rodek had been COO of FedEx; he knew what these people really needed and could truly talk the talk.

The concept was simple, easy to understand, and easy to talk about. Still, the group decided not to use it.

Instead, the focus turned toward more traditional advertising and public relations by concentrating on the technology story. Although the company succeeded quite well under Rodek's leadership, the marketing committee killed the COO conversation platform, worrying that it was too simple in view of the depth and complexity of the company's technology.

Much later, two of the people from the committee e-mailed me: "We should have used the COO idea. People would have gotten our story much faster."

There are nine topics, as explained in Chapter 5, that people most like to talk about: beliefs and aspirations, David vs. Goliath stories, avalanches about to roll, anxieties, counterintuitive/ contrarian perspectives, personalities and personal stories, how-to, glitz and glam, and ideas associated with seasonal events.

3. Make it someone's job—and hold that person accountable

Conversational marketing doesn't cost millions or require hiring specialized agencies. It does, however, have to be added to the marketing organization—to job descriptions, for example, and to how employees are rewarded. The point is that if conversational marketing isn't made part of people's jobs, it won't happen.

Conversational marketing starts by having something interesting to talk about, something that piques customers' interest and helps them better understand what your company is all about. To make sure the conversations help people understand your views and you theirs, the first step is to make sure conversations make meaning, not buzz.

Chapter 2 shows you how to become a meaning maker.

Chapter 2

Make meaning, not buzz

The problem in making decisions today isn't a lack of information. The problem is trying to make sense of so much information amid so much sterile, all-about-us marketing information. If you want people to listen to you, don't think of yourself as a content producer or an information distributor. Be a meaning maker, not a buzz maker.

Organizations that help customers make sense of an abundance of choices become trusted advisers and sources to which people turn. This chapter explains:

* Why people want meaning, not buzz
* Why a goal of marketing—and of a marketing conversation—is to create understanding, and how "meaning making" helps accomplish this goal
* The four ingredients of meaning making are context, relevancy, pattern making, and emotion
* How adults make meaning with a five-year-old mind, and what this means to marketing

Overwhelmed and desperately seeking meaning

What if everyone is talking about a company, product, or issue, but the talk leads nowhere? No sales increase. No tick in market share. No big wins. That's what often happens with buzz-marketing programs and glitzy, attention-grabbing advertising campaigns.

There was a lot of buzz about the Segway scooter, but sales fell flat. Burger King's "Subservient Chicken" campaign was talked about all over the Internet and at real-world watercoolers, but the buzz didn't increase sales of Burger King chicken products.

Presidential hopeful Howard Dean ramped up the political buzz machine a few years back, but he still failed to win the Democratic nomination.

Too often, short-term buzz and awareness lead to a business dead end. It's entertaining but it's like eating cotton candy—novel, fun, but in a couple hours you're hungry for real food. Or buzz is just flat-out wrong for the product category, such as marketing a complex, expensive business-to-business product or service that could never be considered "cool."

It's not buzz or more information that people want; it's meaning. My health insurance company recently ran television ads announcing a new plan for small businesses and then sent me a large packet of information about the new plan, my current plan, and all the other available plans. I was interested in this information because the price of my existing health insurance was increasing 32 percent that year, putting the monthly insurance bill over $1,000. But darned if I could figure out the right health plan to choose for my family. I couldn't figure out the differences among my existing plan, the new plan, and all the other plans—aside from their having different names and different price tags. I couldn't figure out which was more relevant to our family needs, or the trade-off in services and deductibles. I was overwhelmed, annoyed, and frustrated. There was so much information, so many facts—yet so little meaning.

The social and economic issues in Africa are far more complex than my health plan, yet I have a better grasp of those issues because of a rock musician who is also a highly effective meaning maker. Have you ever heard U2's Bono talk about his DATA organization, which is dedicated to reducing debt, increasing trade, and treating AIDS in Africa? He has an astute command of the facts around the issues and talks about them with a genuine passion that draws you into the discussion, making you want to learn more about some complex and substantive issues and, yes, maybe even donate money or time to the cause.

Bono has framed the issues in ways that are relevant to world leaders, business executives, U2 fans, and even highly skeptical politicians and evangelical Christians.

"[O]f evangelicals polled in 2000, only 6 percent felt it incumbent upon them to respond to the AIDS emergency," he explained in a PBS *Frontline* interview.[1] "I was deeply offended by that, so I asked to meet with as many church leaders as I could, and used examples from the Scriptures. . . . I argued . . . 'Isn't this what Christ spent his time with?' "

When Bono met with ultraconservative U.S. Senator Jesse Helms, his conversation focused on discussing AIDS in a way that would be most meaningful to Helms. " 'I started talking about Scripture. I talked about AIDS as the leprosy of our age.' Finally the flinty old Southerner rose to his feet, grabbed for his cane, and said, 'I want to give you a blessing.' "[2]

Using meaning-making techniques, Bono talks about the issues with an urgent relevancy and emotional wallop. He helps to speed public understanding as well as policy decisions.

When a fan complimented Bono on his cause, Bono corrected him. "'I don't think 6,000 Africans a day dying from AIDS is a cause, it's an *emergency*."[3]

Now *that's* something meaningful to talk about.

Meaning helps make sense of information

Meaning making helps *makes sense* of an idea, concept, or product, showing us how it relates to what we already know and believe. Like Bono helping Jesse Helms understand the urgency of AIDS in Africa by talking about how it was like leprosy for the New Age.

Although buzz or advertising may spark interest, meaning making builds understanding. Meaning making grounds conversations, helping people to comprehend information and to make decisions on rational and emotional levels.

Eric Jensen, a brain-based learning expert and the author of *Teaching with the Brain in Mind*, believes that meaning is more important than information because the brain is meaning-driven.

That's why meaning making is such a powerful concept for leadership, sales, marketing, customer relationship building, and activism.

Great leaders in all fields—from Gandhi and Margaret Thatcher to GE's Jack Welch and Ford Motors' Jacques Nasser—have been meaning makers, helping people to make sense of new concepts.

In fact, the more innovative or disruptive the idea or product, the greater the need for a meaning-maker approach to communications.

"We believe the need for meaning and a sense for order is universal," state Harvard Business School professors Joel M. Podolny, Rakesh Khurana, and Marya Hill-Popper in the Harvard Business School's *Working Knowledge* article "How to Put Meaning Back into Leading." According to the business professors, "It is a need that is deeply linked to the definition of what it means to be human. Without meaning, individuals tend to become rigid and hollow. Organizational life seems petty and zero sum. People go through the motions, and do so amid distrust, cynicism, indifference, and a sense of alienation."[4]

Adapt the Harvard professors' management view of meaning making and apply it to marketing and we can understand that without meaning, customers tend to become skeptical and indifferent. Advertising seems petty and zero sum. Customers go through the motions and do so amid distrust, cynicism, indifference, and a sense of alienation.

In talking about his fascination with meaning making, George Siemens, instructor at Red River College in Winnipeg, Canada, says, "Knowing something is great. Knowing what it means moves us to a level where we can act—to support, change, redirect, challenge."[5]

In other words, meaning making speeds action because it speeds understanding; it helps get people to buy our products, use our services, and support our issues. Without helping people make sense of information, much of that information will be overlooked, misunderstood, taken out of context, or tossed aside.

Consider the 2006 Medicare Drug Plan, the biggest expansion of Medicare since the health care program began. Information explaining the new prescription drug benefits for senior citizens is so complex and confusing that nearly 80 percent of the people eligible for the benefit said they don't know whether or not they will sign up.

"It's so complex that churches, senior centers, and school auditoriums are filling with seniors attending information sessions and asking the same question: What do I do now?" according to *The Cincinnati Post*.[6]

Private health insurance companies stepped in to try to better explain the program, but many seniors considered their marketing efforts superficial, or worse. "The health plans have filled the vacuum with glossy marketing brochures, some of which are flagrantly misleading," said *Los Angles Times* columnist Michael Hiltzik.[7]

Efforts to market the Medicare Drug Plan have achieved widespread awareness, yet they lack meaning and understanding. So the marketing has failed.

At the 2004 American Association of Advertising Agencies Conference, Procter & Gamble global marketing officer Jim Stengel talked about how the old model of marketing was broken. "Now is the time for all of us to push our thinking further," he said. "Marketing pitches can be made meaningful for your consumer, not meaningless."[8]

Four meaning-making ingredients—relevancy, emotion, context, and pattern making

Our brains innately seek meaning by looking for and connecting with patterns of information. The patterns and connections help us to see value in information we may otherwise ignore as meaningless. Our job as marketers is to help people see the patterns, to help them connect with ideas.

Pat Wolfe, author of *Brain Matters: Translating Research into*

Classroom Practice, explains, "Neural networks 'check out' sensory stimuli as soon as they enter the brain to see if they form a familiar pattern. If they do, a match occurs, and the brain determines that the new stimuli are familiar. In this case, we could say that the new information makes sense or has meaning. What happens if there is no match? The brain may attend to the meaningless information for a short period of time because it is novel; but if it can make no sense out of the incoming stimuli, the brain will probably not process them further."[9]

Brain-based learning experts have found that the four factors in making meaning are relevancy, emotions, context, and pattern making. "Relevance is a function of the brain making a connection from existing neural sites," says brain-based learning expert Eric Jensen. "Emotions are triggered by the brain's chemistry, and context triggers pattern making that may be related to the formation or activation of larger neural fields. All meaning making has at least one of those ingredients."[10]

To make meaning, we want to know the following:

* How does a topic relate to the bigger picture? How does it fit with our view of the industry issues? (We need to fit information into context and existing frameworks of understanding.)
* What does this mean to me, to my company, and to our situation? (Meaning must be relevant.)
* How do the dots connect with other pieces of the issue? What are the best practices? What are the criteria for success? What lessons have been learned from failures? (Our brains want to see patterns and connect ideas in some way.)
* How does it make me feel? Do I feel smarter by knowing this? Do I feel more confident in making a recommendation to my boss? Do I trust the company more? Do I feel that working with the company would be more enjoyable than my other

available choices? (Emotion is the superhighway of understanding and making meaning.)

Context and pattern making: Connecting the dots within a larger frame

An idea will be meaningful only if it relates to the listener's experience. In other words, to help a customer understand a new
concept or why to believe in a company, relate the company's
ideas to the customer's previous experiences and perceptions of
the industry.

We have to remember that we're not operating in a vacuum.
Customers are forming their ideas from multiple sources, including competitors, financial and industry analysts, and the
media. It's helpful to step back and ask, "What arena are our
customers operating in and how do our company ideas relate
within that arena?" If we ignore the customer's frame of reference, the customer will ignore us.

After World War II, one of Winston Churchill's generals remarked to the prime minister that his inspiring speeches helped
bring about victory. Churchill replied that he had only said what
was in people's hearts. In other words, he was speaking to meanings that already existed. He was connecting meanings in new
ways, in the context of what the British already believed about
war and Hitler.

Examples of companies trying to fit themselves into a broader
context include fast-food companies talking about their products
and values in the context of healthy eating, carmakers talking
about hybrid vehicles in the context of being less dependent on
gas and being better stewards of the environment, and insurance

providers talking about long-term care in the context of aging and health care policy. Today, public policy is framed in the context of security and the war against global terrorism.

As you can see, marketing *anything* requires explaining ideas within people's existing frames of reference—that is, in a context they already understand.

For example, to fend off more controls, the tobacco industry has astutely framed its position on smoking in the context of American values. Smoking is an individual right, the tobacco companies claim, and the public health community is trying to take that right away. Whether you agree or disagree with this strategy, it's a good example of how to market within an existing context.

Talking out of context is usually fruitless. After the French voted "non" and the Dutch followed with a "nay" on the European Union constitution in 2005, many policy experts, journalists, and politicians began to dissect what happened. One of the biggest issues was that the voters just didn't understand what the EU constitution would mean to them. It wasn't communicated within their frame of reference.

The pro-Union policymakers and politicians that had holed up in Brussels, diligently researching and writing dense, rhetoric-filled papers documenting the economic and political policy benefits of a more united Europe, didn't effectively market the benefits of the constitution within the context of voters' lives. Voters wanted to know how the constitution would allow them to maintain their national identities. In giving up control over things like immigration policy, how would they maintain their Dutch or French culture?

When talking on National Public Radio's *The Connection* program, Jocelyne Cesari, visiting associate professor at Harvard's

Center for Middle East Studies and Divinity School, underscored the communications problem by stating, "Up until now the European Union has been seen as a bureaucratic process. When people say 'Brussels' they mean a very specialized place—writing treaties of thirty pages long with technical features. People in Europe didn't understand what the story would be for them in this new union. This is very important. It is the responsibility of all national political classes to make a story that resonates."[11]

Contexts in business and government are shifting more quickly than ever. Understanding the context in which we're discussing ideas is essential; otherwise we will end up just talking to ourselves.

Related to context is how patterns are formed within the frame of reference. Pattern making involves seeing relationships among ideas and connecting ideas within the context.

One reason we enjoy hearing about best practices, observations, secrets, and lessons is that someone is pulling together and connecting different bits of information in a meaningful pattern that fits into a context we already understand.

The following quick look at some of the best-selling self-help and business books proves this point: *1,000 Places to See Before You Die* by Patricia Schultz; *The Seven Habits of Highly Effective People* by Stephen R. Covey; *The 48 Laws of Power* by Robert Greene and Joost Elffers; *The Five Dysfunctions of a Team* by Patrick Lencioni; *Secrets of the Millionaire Mind* by T. Harv Eker; *A Life in Balance: Nourishing the Four Roots of True Happiness* by Dr. Kathleen Hall; and *96 Great Interview Questions to Ask Before You Hire* by Paul Falcone.

For marketers, observing patterns—and sharing lessons learned—is a great way to help customers because their minds are innately seeking out patterns. The old business adage, "We need to connect the dots," is spot on.

Being relevant: Beyond acts of God and Congress

Congress enacted the Sarbanes Oxley Act of 2002 to tighten up compliance and financial disclosure rules for major companies and to build back investor confidence after financial scandals at major corporations such as Enron, WorldCom, and Tyco.

It was also a gift to many business analytic software companies because it made their products especially relevant to customers. Companies like SAS Institute and Hyperion created highly effective marketing programs to suggest ways that their software products provide the financial and operational data the law now requires.

Another example to consider is the boom in business for security companies after 9/11 or for construction and engineering firms following Hurricane Katrina. The heightened relevancy makes their marketing much easier.

But what if there's no act of God—or act of Congress? You'll have to find relevant hooks to connect the views. There is no worse insult to CEOs and marketers than hearing, "You're just not relevant." (Excepting, of course, its first cousin, "You're out of touch with your customers.")

A management consultant firm asked me to review a new service it was developing to teach executives the value of a business strategy and ways to create one. The workbooks, audio programs, and workshop format were thorough, rich in content, and professionally produced. But they were unappealing.

"Why is this especially relevant for today's executives?" I asked the firm's managing partner. "Why should they pay attention to strategy now, instead of, say, figuring out how to change financial systems to comply with Sarbanes Oxley?"

He replied, "Every executive can be more effective by knowing how to more systematically develop business strategy." I'm sure this is true, but there was nothing to talk about to help market the service. There was no especially relevant reason for people to want to care.

Even consumer-friendly topics need to be infused with relevancy. I serve on a board of a major regional theater and often remind the staff that it needs to give people a relevant reason to see a play, other than fine acting, great directing, lots of laughs, and the fact that it's a classic. Why is a particular play so relevant that you really must see it?

Here's an e-mail message showing the progression from merely explaining a play to finding relevant ways to talk about it.

```
> -----Original Message-----
> Hamlet by William Shakespeare directed by
  Brian McEleney In
> January/February in the Chace Theater
>
> Shakespeare's masterpiece, probably the
  most performed play in the
> world, has never been seen at Trinity—hard
  to believe! Everyone,
> beginners to veterans, should see this play.
> What is it about?
> Hamlet is the prince of Denmark. His uncle
  poisons his father, marries
> his mother, and takes the throne. Hamlet
  must decide how, and if, to
> take revenge.
> Is it "traditional Shakespeare"?
```

Our approach to Hamlet is traditional but never in tights and doublets—think of our *Othello, Henry IV,* and *Henry V.* In *Hamlet,* the costumes look like the 1930s, reminiscent of *Gosford Park* and *The Remains of the Day.*

```
> The nontraditional thing here is that the
  role of Polonius will be
> played as a woman, by company actress
  Janice Duclos. Polonius is the
> parent of Ophelia and Laertes . . .
  "Neither a borrower nor a lender
> be . . . to thine own self be true."
  Trinity has a long history of
> casting across gender, when one of our
  talented actors can bring
> something exciting to the role.
```

The e-mail simply explained the production; there was no hook to why *now.* So I asked:

```
> Why is Hamlet—or this production of it—
  especially relevant today? Why is it urgent
  for people to see it?
```

The communications director's following reply gave me something to talk about:

```
> Some thoughts from the director—Brian sees
  Hamlet as an arrogant, careless
> rich kid. The play will be set in the 1930s
  showing a glamorous, corrupt world with
  distinct class separation.
```

Class separation and the struggles of arrogant rich kids—now, that's more relevant and conversation worthy. It also helped make this production of *Hamlet* meaningful to audiences.

Here's another example of adding relevancy. Consider that you are marketing a commodity like milk and trying to get more adults to drink it. How do you make it more relevant? The "Got Milk" people focused on how consuming more dairy helps you lose weight. According to the www.got-milk.com Web site: "A growing body of research shows that when cutting calories to lose weight, including three servings of milk, cheese, or yogurt each day helps people burn more fat and lose more weight than just cutting calories alone."[12] By making milk relevant to the people interested in losing weight, The Got-Milk organization found new ways to talk about milk.

Procter & Gamble originally thought that its Febreze brand, which removes odors from fabrics, would be most relevant to people who wanted to remove smoke from their clothes. But by asking, "Who is this relevant to?" the marketers found that the brand was meaningful to people who wanted to remove odors from other places—smelly gym bags, teenagers' closets, and the backseats of cars. After P&G changed the way it promoted Febreze—from odor remover to fabric refresher—the business grew by about 50 percent over the past three years.[13] People other than smokers want to know how to make things smell good.

One note about relevancy: Sometimes we become too attached to the products and services we're marketing. So we need to always step back from time to time and understand our customers' point of view—what is relevant *to them*? (Chapter 7 provides seven ways to do this.) The more people see the relevancy connection, the greater the likelihood that they will find the conversation meaningful.

Love this: Emotion is the superhighway to meaning

Our brains are hardwired to respond to emotions and feelings. Even more important, emotions strongly influence whether a person will believe or take action.

Impassioned pleas not to drink and drive from a mother whose child has died in a drunk-driving accident are more compelling than reading a list of facts about drunk driving. An executive who exudes passion will more easily get people to listen, understand, and follow.

"CEOs shouldn't be afraid to talk to their people in an emotional way, about what they really feel and how they really think," former Southwest Airlines CEO Herb Kelleher once remarked.

Interestingly, however, emotion is often considered something you don't do in business. Successful businesspeople—so goes the theory—are polished, articulate, crisp, and emotionless. It is all right to use emotion in advertisements and human resources training programs, but when you come to work, kindly check your emotions at the door.

But—big surprise—that business assumption is wrong. No emotion—too little passion—stunts communications; it bores rather than engages. Even worse, people may misinterpret sterile communications, thinking that management just doesn't care.

Emotion isn't to be feared. Consider the emotive styles of Kelleher and former CEO of General Electric Jack Welch, who created more shareholder wealth than any other CEO. Aside from achieving extraordinary financial returns, these executives exuded passion and peppered their conversations with "love," the word that most executives avoid like the plague.

"A company is stronger if it's bound more by love than fear,"

Kelleher said.[14] In fact, the airline's tag line for many years was, "The airline that love built."

Jack Welch, who also liberally uses the L word in conversations, believes that passion is a crucial trait for success in business. He has often said that passion is the first quality in an "A" player. "By passion, I mean a heartfelt, deep and authentic excitement about work. People with passion care—really care in their bones—about colleagues, employees, and friends winning. They love to learn and grow."[15]

Our brains tune into emotion to figure out whether we should pay attention, whether someone believes what he or she is saying, and whether we should trust people or disregard them. This is why talking about what you believe in is so important. If you are not connected emotionally with what you are talking about, people will disconnect. If you don't care about the idea, neither will they. Screenwriting coach Robert McKee explained to *Harvard Business Review's* Bronwyn Fryer: "A big part of a CEO's job is to motivate people to reach certain goals. The first [way to do that] is by using conventional rhetoric, which is what most executives are trained in. . . . [A] much more powerful way . . . is by uniting an idea with an emotion."[16]

This is why using points of view to engage people in conversations can be so effective. Points of view are not just rational facts, but ideas laden with emotional beliefs. In other words, the point of view in and of itself provokes an emotionally charged conversation.

Beyond ideas and words, we humans also make judgments based on *how* people talk. We innately tune into the emotions and attitudes of the person when listening. We often make snap judgments without consciously factoring in the words being spoken. To show the effect of these social signals, researchers at the Massachusetts Institute of Technology have studied people's reactions during conversations. Using a social perception machine that measures social signals in conversations—but not the words themselves—MIT researchers can predict, after just a few minutes of listening and with almost 90 percent accuracy, outcomes such as these:

* Who would exchange business cards at a meeting
* Which couples would exchange phone numbers at a bar
* Who would come out ahead in a negotiation
* Subjective judgments, including whether a person felt a negotiation was honest and fair, or a conversation interesting

"What is surprising is that the largely subconscious social signaling that occurs at the start of the interaction appears to be more predictive than either the contextual facts (attractiveness and experience) or the linguistic structure (strategy chosen, arguments used) and so on," says Professor Alex (Sandy) Pentland, who directs the Human Dynamics research group at the MIT Media Lab.[17] "Moreover, the decisions we examined are among the most important in life: finding a mate, getting a job, negotiating a salary, and finding a place in a social network. These are activities for which humans prepare intellectually and strategically for decades."

In other words, we often make snap decisions based just on the tone and emotion in someone's voice. Even if someone has thoroughly prepared reasoned and logical arguments, we make judgments based more on the social signals during the conversation than on the content of the words. Therefore, if a CEO is talking with a group of employees or customers and he or she really isn't interested in the conversation, the listeners will know it. People can sniff out insincerity or lack of interest in minutes, according to the MIT research.

Consider, for instance, what happened when the CEO of a multibillion dollar conglomerate spoke to his company's annual "Communications Council" meeting, where the communications directors of various subsidiaries come together for a few days to talk about communications issues, how to improve corporate-wide processes, and then listen to an outside expert or two.

To open the meeting the CEO called in on speakerphone. "Gee," we thought, "this guy really must consider communications important to the business. He's running a multibillion-dollar corporation but he's making time for his communications managers. What a great thing for these people to have an enlightened CEO."

Then he started talking, saying all the right words, but in a rather pat and glib style. Within two minutes, we knew his commitment to communications was lip service. "Communicate more" was just an item on his to-do list. He probably understood, intellectually, why managers need to communicate more clearly and openly with employees. However, his lack of emotion and the disingenuousness tone in his voice gave him away.

After his fifteen-minute chat, no one in the room was particularly fired up or motivated to talk about his remarks. They didn't believe what he said because he didn't believe it. Rather than motivating these people and building his leadership credibility, he sent another message: "What you communications folks are doing isn't all that important to me."

In fact, the only time that he got somewhat fired up during his scripted fireside chat was when he warned about the need to be especially cautious in communicating. "With Sarbanes Oxley and SEC rules about information disclosure, we need to be especially careful about what we disclose and to whom," he stressed. "This is why we need to be so careful about communicating. We—particularly me—could go to jail if we make a mistake."[18]

If people aren't interested in what they're talking about, how are they going to talk to customers, analysts, media, and employees in any meaningful way? They're not. Faking it, as the social signaling experts have shown, rarely works. If we talk about something we don't believe in, people ignore us and maybe even lose confidence in us. Faked emotion contributes as much to meaning making as genuine emotion and not in a positive way. The passion and conviction of our beliefs triggers emotion, the most potent meaning-making ingredient.

Meaning-making lessons for the five-year-old mind in all of us

One last note about meaning making is that adults make meaning with their five-year-old minds, and this has some practical implications to marketing practices.

Everything we know wasn't learned in kindergarten, but how we learn most things is remarkably similar to how five-year-olds learn. This is true whether you're a forty-nine-year-old PhD or a twenty-year-old assembly-line worker.

"I stand by my major claim that the mind of the five-year-old persists in most of us, in most of our daily activities, with only the disciplinary expert escaping fully from its powerful clutches in certain areas of expertise," says Howard Gardner, education professor at Harvard University and author of *Leading Minds: An Anatomy of Leadership.*[19]

In studying leaders, Gardner found that, as a rule, experts—scientists, artists, or accountants—who lead others in their specialized field lead directly through their work. They can go deep into their subject matter area because their audiences share the same deep specialization.

But people who lead, or market to, a more heterogeneous group lead through communication, particularly through stories and conversations. This type of leadership involves tapping into the five-year-old that lives in each of us. And that five-year-old learns largely through conversations.

As marketers we often forget that many audiences are not specialists, but more heterogeneous. Examples of this include marketing drugs to consumers rather than physicians, accounting software to small business owners instead of accountants, John Deere tractors to suburbanites versus experienced farmers, or expensive enterprise software to senior executives instead of IT specialists.

Here's a look at how a five-year-old learns and what that means to marketing practices:

* Likes to argue and reason; uses words like "because": *Explain why and why not.*
* Uses five to eight words in a sentence: *Keep it brief; use short sentences.*
* Is interested in cause and effect: *Explain, "if we do this, then this is what will happen. If we don't do this, then here are the likely consequences."*
* Understands and uses comparative terms: *Analogies help understanding.*
* Enjoys creating and telling stories: *Storytelling remains one of the best ways to make meaning and help people remember, understand, and repeat ideas.*
* Uses swear words to get attention: *Disruptive ideas and language get attention.*

* Likes to try new things: *People get bored and like new ideas and experiences.*
* Likes simple rules: *Don't make things too complicated or impose too many new "musts."*
* Has a good sense of humor: *Keep a perspective; lighten up.*

In explaining how he picks successful children's books like *Harry Potter,* Barry Cunningham, publisher of Chicken House Children's Books, says that he taps into the child within him, which might be good advice for marketers as they seek to become meaning makers. "If you carry the child within you, that's what works. You need a real ability to feel the hope, wonder, burning sense of injustice, fear, or rage of childhood—an unfettered mind that still dreams, that goes with the truth of a story."[20]

Marketing needs more meaning, because as people try to digest more information and more choices, they want help in sorting it all out so that they can make a decision. They want to know what is relevant within their frame of reference, and they want genuine advice. This is why so many of us turn to our peers for help. It's also why a marketing goal is to make our companies sources that customers want to turn to for help. By helping customers better understand and make meaning, our companies become trusted sources, not just promoters to whom customers may or may not listen.

One of the best ways to reach out to customers and begin the meaning-making process is to have a point of view that provokes discussion around ideas that are relevant to customers, fit within their frame of context, and move them emotionally. Chapter 3 explains points of view and shows how three very different organizations use them in conversational marketing programs.

Chapter 3

Have a fresh point of view (or several)

To stand out in our cluttered, noisy, skeptical world, we need a singular perspective—a point of view—that distinguishes us and helps people better understand our companies and products; that evokes conversation and makes it easy for people to talk to other people about our companies. This chapter will:

* Explain what a point of view is and how it differs from traditional marketing basics like mission statements, value propositions, messages, and elevator speeches
* Show how too many packaged messages but no discernible point of view can make a good company sound irrelevant
* Take an inside look at the points of view and conversational marketing programs of three different organizations: Sun Microsystems, Unilever's Dove brand, and Women & Infants Hospital

> ### A point of view sets you apart, speeds understanding, and provokes conversation

A point of view is a perspective that often evokes conversation. When we talk about our points of view, we begin with phrases like, "The way I see it . . ." or "What I've learned about . . ." or "From my perspective . . ." And in that context, we talk about our beliefs. Hopefully, when people hear your point of view, they say, "That's interesting. Tell me more." And even if they disagree, they may see things from a new point of view or get involved in talking about the ideas.

This active involvement helps companies learn more about customers, and helps customers learn more about the company in ways that help form bonds and lead to action. Involvement is a prerequisite to action, whether that action is changing a perception, deciding to buy, or adopting new beliefs and behaviors.

Having a point of view can help an organization stand for more than more of the same—and talk about ideas that help people get to know what the company is all about. People might not agree with your point of view, but they won't ignore it either. As comedian Lily Tomlin once joked, "I always wanted to be somebody. Now I know I should have been more specific."

Here are some specific points of view:

* "We believe software is too complex—too many features, too many buttons, too much to learn. We build the best Web-based software products with *the least number of features*. Our products do less than the competition—intentionally," claims 37signals, a Chicago-based software company that makes dead-simple Web offerings.

* "When we talk to other people about Southwest Airlines, I always tell them that it's got to *come from the heart* not from the head. It has to be spontaneous, it has to be sincere, it has to be emotional," says Herb Kelleher, executive chairman of the board, Southwest Airlines.[1]

* Although many people see Starbucks as a fancy coffee shop, its chairman Howard Schultz sees the eight-thousand-store chain as a "third place" for people to hang out at in addition to home and work.[2]

* "People feel like a rowboat bobbing in the ocean, but they could be more of an ocean liner if they would *diversify their assets, make a plan, and follow it*," says Charles Schwab, chairman of Charles Schwab.[3]

* "Our collective generation believes the desktop PC is the most important thing to give to people. *I don't buy that*. The most important thing to give is access to the Internet," says Jonathan Schwartz, president, Sun Microsystems.[4]

* What makes the Ellen Tracy clothing line different? "What's worked for Ellen Tracy for more than 50 years is the consistency of making apparel that elicits a '*Wow, she's well dressed,*'" explains George Sharp, vice president of design, Ellen Tracy.[5]

A fresh point of view (or several) glues together programs, engages people in discussions, and liberates the marketing staff. A point of view is easy to understand, to remember, and to talk about in our own words. With a fresh point of view, people in and around the company suddenly have interesting things to talk about with customers (or the media, analysts, or employees).

The purpose of a point of view is to help people understand what an organization is actually all about. It shapes people's feelings about whether to work with us, buy from us, or invest in us. It's meant to provoke thinking and conversation versus explaining a product or capability or documenting vision, mission, values, or value proposition.

Although much has been written about the value of having a marketing story (see Seth Godin's book *All Marketers Are Liars* as an example), a story is of little value if it's not connected to a point of view. Stories are told to make a point.

"We may have forgotten the stories, but we remember the point," explains Joe Lambert of the *Digital Storytelling Cookbook*. "In *King Lear* the point or central premise is 'blind trust leads to destruction.' In *Macbeth*, it is 'unbridled greed leads to destruction.' Every part of the dramatic action can be boiled down to serving these points of view."[6]

Similarly, marketing programs and communications can be simplified by making them serve a company or a brand's point of view.

The "so what" introduction of the new CA

When John Swainson took over as CEO of Computer Associates (CA), he had quite a bit of business cleaning up to do. He knew that he needed to reposition the company to hold on to customers and try to win new ones.

He hired Madison Avenue's top marketing strategy, branding, advertising, and public relations firms and put them to work to tell the story of the new organization he was leading. He had received positive feedback in conversations with customers, analysts, and reporters when he explained his strategy for the new Computer Associates, to be called simply CA. The strategy was to be highly ethical, focused on developing technology products that added real value for customers, and be earnestly committed to making it easier to do business with CA.

A straight-shooting, plain-talking kind of guy, Swainson felt the company was now ready to tell its new story to the business industry.

The message makers, advertising masters, branding gurus, and spin doctors went to work, spent millions, and introduced the new CA to the world in grand style—full-page advertisements in business media; lavish customer parties in Las Vegas; press briefings; and a newly designed Web site, logo, and tag line.

People who heard Swainson himself explain the new strategy paid attention and opened their minds to the possibility that CA might have a chance to come back. But the rest of us who read the ads, went to the new Web site, or scanned the press releases had a hard time figuring out what CA was talking about. Darned if even my savviest technology executive friends could see things from CA's point of view.

The shallow ads demonstrated a lack of connection with market conversations. "Remember when technology had the power to inspire you? Believe again," said the headlines. Come on. Most of us techies never thought that technology had become less inspiring. CA, however, may have lost *its* inspiration along the way, which accounted for so little innovation and growth.

But we customers don't need to be told in ads to "believe again" in technology. What we need to be told is why we should believe again in CA and *its* technology.

Read more of CA's marketing and you're right back into all-about-me product information, expounding on its new vision of Enterprise IT Management (EITM), designed to "unify and simplify complex IT environments across the enterprise." But hello, what exactly is it? I know technology, yet I can't figure out what the big "aha!" is here.

Read further and see more trite lines and tired talk, much of which was used by other tech companies in the 1990s, such as "transforming business," "unifying and simplifying complex IT environments," "reach a higher order of IT," "simplify the complex," "deliver fully against your business goals." Say what?

I've heard Swainson talk. He's engaging and direct, which is why this marketing campaign is especially painful. Why didn't he talk about his fresh ideas for growth, in his own words—not a copywriter's? CA must have a point of view on enterprise technology that is contrarian, counterintuitive, unusual, insightful, or surprising. Also something other than money must be motivating Swainson and his team to take on the work of turning around a troubled $3.5 billion global company. He should have talked about those ideas—in words real people use.

A new logo and name change don't matter all that much today. Customers want to connect with the company and its people—not with a new acronym. They want to talk about new ideas. More than anything, people want a reason to believe in you. Give it to them straight up and help them understand the point and the beliefs behind that point.

If people don't understand a company's point of view and have a hard time making sense of all the marketing and sales materials, they often begin to suspect that perhaps there is no real strategy. "It's not us," they realize, "it's them. The new logo and ad campaigns are attempts to hide the fact that the strategy is weak."

Ten characteristics of a point of view

Not only do points of view help people to talk and to engage in meaningful discussions, but they help connect people with ideas and concepts that help them better understand the company. Here is a review of ten characteristics of effective points of view. The first four are essential; the remaining six are good to have because they strengthen a point of view.

1. Engaging

An effective point of view evokes the response, "That's kind of interesting. Tell me more." It starts conversations rather than just informing. People want to know more and to offer their views as well.

2. True

Marketers can support a point of view with facts, trend information, aggregated insights, or other data. The more evidence there is to support a point of view, the greater the likelihood that people will accept it as credible.

3. Relevant

The more relevant the idea to the intended audience, the more interested people will be. A sixty-year-old will find discussions about long-term health care insurance and Social Security far more interesting than a twenty-year-old will.

4. Genuine

The organization has to believe in the idea—truly. Otherwise talking about it will be difficult, stilted, boring, hollow, and empty. People have a sixth sense for picking up on whether others really mean what they're saying. There is no faking it. Either believe in it, or find something that you actually *do* care about.

5. Fresh

The view is different and new from most conversations around the topic. We all are probably guilty of defaulting to the latest industry "big idea," and talking about it so much that no one wants to hear about it anymore. Sometimes, however, the point of view doesn't need to be original and new. It simply needs to be framed and expressed in a new way, helping people to discover and talk about its other important aspects.

6. Connects the dots

A point of view should somehow connect to the business vision or strategy. It may be about practical aspects of your strategy (for example, why increasing prices 25 percent will help open new markets more quickly). Or it may be about building trust and relationships so people will feel good about doing business with the company—a prerequisite for nearly any strategic success. Connect the dots—the point of view to the strategy—otherwise it's just talk.

7. Memorable

Does the point of view stick in a person's head? Is it easy to remember? The view should be so simple and straightforward—in concept and in words—that there is no need for elaborate talking points, long explanatory documents, or in-depth training sessions so people can "get it."

8. "Talkable"

Is it easy for people to talk about the concept in their own words and tell their own stories around it? Does it jump-start two-way talk?

9. Leggy

Does the idea resonate with multiple audiences, through multiple communications channels? The more legs a point of view has, the more you can build marketing and sales programs around it, so the talk adds up.

10. Likeable

Do people like talking about your point of view? Is it so inspiring, provocative, brave, or bold that they naturally jump into conversations about it?

> ## How a point of view differs from vision, value proposition, messages, and elevator speeches

In marketing, a point of view from which we express ideas and beliefs is a fundamental element to be added to conventional fundamentals like vision, mission, value proposition statements, elevator speeches, and messaging documents. A point of view is an "also," not an "instead of."

The purpose of these conventional fundamentals is not to engage people in interesting conversations. They are directional, informative documents—more like maps and blueprints than motivational guides. They're about the company's intentions and objectives. Most are written to be read—not to be talked about or to spark meaningful debate or conversation.

"A vision is an inspirational statement of what you expect to do with the company or the brand," explains Kevin Clancy, former marketing professor and CEO of the global marketing strategy firm Copernicus. "The mission is the operational prescription for what you need to do to accomplish the vision.

The positioning is simply a one- or two-sentence statement that is not about vision or not about mission as such, but is a message you want to imprint in the minds of customers and prospects. It is about your brand, product, or service, and how it is different from—and therefore better than—the competition's."[7] Note that the focus is about the product or brand; these conventional statements are more *us*-focused than *other*-focused.

Vision	Why the organization exists; provides direction to what the company does
Mission	The action plan for accomplishing the vision
Values	Shared values, guiding behavior, and actions
Customer value proposition	Describes the value customers realize from doing business with the company or brand
Elevator speech	Simple sentence describing what the business is and how it differs from its competitors
Messaging	Most important points to convey about the company, product, or program
Point of view	Beliefs and ideas that help build understanding, provoke conversation—*and* are something a person would actually say

Think about corporate vision, mission, value proposition, and elevator speeches. How often do people talk about the mission statement with customers? When was the last time someone had a great conversation about the company's values? How often do we go back to these documents to shape our thinking around a conversation we'll be having with customers or analysts? Not often.

When friends ask, "Hey, what's new with ABC corporation?" do you talk about the corporate values and recite the vision?

How jazzed are you when using the elevator speech? (Do any of us ever really use it?)

It's not that these documents are bad (although many say very little), it's that they're not intended to help us talk. Another problem with these documents is that creating them usually involves a tedious, drawn-out committee task, leaving participants almost as lifeless as the language in the statements. Management puts the documents on the Web and Intranets, prints them in little handbooks, and posts Ten Commandment–like posters in the hallways. Then hardly anyone pays attention to them until there's a new CEO, a merger, or the five-year plan calls for an update. That's why you can't rely on these documents for communications purposes.

They are only the beginning of marketing. If your marketing doesn't lead to some sort of dialogue with customers and market influencers, it's not effective marketing.

After completing fundamentals like targeting and positioning, the marketer's next job is to extract points of view from the organization that will generate conversations, which will help people to better understand an issue, a product, a business situation, or a company strategy.

How does the American Canadian Caribbean cruise line differ from all the other cruise ships? Since founding the company in 1966, Luther Blount's point of view was that cruising on one of his ships should feel like "sailing on your friend's yacht." And he firmly believed that passengers' money is better spent on getting to exciting nontouristy destinations than on "unnecessary frills" that other cruises offer.[8]

Sometimes a point of view captures a fresh take on industry issues, emerging trends, or common obstacles. Other times it is directly connected to the company's vision and value proposition but translated to be more "talkable," interesting, and engaging.

When your company maps out its key messages (sometimes known as *message pyramiding*), make sure its point of view is at the top of the pyramid. (Often, points of view aren't even in the pyramid, with traditional messaging and talking points being all about the company and its products.)

This overarching vocal message should captivate and engage, demonstrating that the company knows the issues so well that it can confidently offer a point of view and discuss that view in friendly, engaging conversations. Companies without articulate points of view are like many well-organized, well-funded political campaigns that lose elections. Attorney James Snyder, speechwriter to Mario Cuomo, the former governor of New York, has said that he's seen many candidates fail because their campaign messages are not engaging. He explains,

> Few in a campaign spend much time thinking about the candidate's complete message. What a mistake. Because when all is said and done, what is actually seen or heard by the voters and media? A candidate speaking. A vocal message that captivates and charms or falls flat on its face and turns voters away in disgust and disappointment.[9]

William Safire, Pulitzer prize–winning journalist, former White House speechwriter, and writer of the *New York Times Magazine* column "On Language," has a similar message in his *Political Dictionary*: "When a candidate does not have his own speech by the end of the campaign, he has not figured out in his own mind what the campaign was really all about."[10]

Same goes for business. What's our own point of view about our industry and our business? What really matters? What doesn't matter? What's important to customers but overlooked by us? What's beginning to emerge that could change the industry? Like a political candidate, we need to figure out our complete message. And that includes our point of view.

Sun Microsystems' point of view — sharing, ending the digital divide

Contrast CA to another big, global high-tech company that stumbled around the same time as CA but has a point of view—Sun Microsystems.

In 2005 Sun faced three challenges. One was that customers and the industry wondered whether the company was still relevant to the high-tech industry. Industry analysts and customers whispered, "Is Sun just a commodity hardware company too late to the open-source software party?"

The second challenge was that every Sun product division aggressively promoted its own products, using conventional feature-benefit product messages. It gave the sales force reams of product information to use with customers. As a result, sales reps had little of substance to discuss with senior-level decision makers.

Why was this? Because those buyers don't want to talk about products; they can have people on their staff look up that information on the Web. They want to talk to the sales reps about issues and trends, what's next in the industry, and what was going on with Sun. "Are you guys going to make it?" Customers aren't just buying technology; they're also buying the company behind the technology products.

The third challenge was that Sun had kissed and made up with long-time rival Microsoft the previous year. For years, Sun chairman Scott McNealy's point of view was pretty much that Microsoft was the evil empire and needed to be destroyed.

So Sun, a company that knew the value of a point of view, had nothing much to talk about, save for new types of servers, software, and grid computing. Everyone in marketing and at the executive level was frustrated. They knew the company was turning around. They believed the company's vision of "the network is the computer" was right. They understood that the new products were good. But something was missing. There was no cause to rally around.

"Scott stopped me in the hall one day and said, 'I think we need to be talking about sharing. How Sun's technology lets users participate in the Internet world and share ideas,'" remembers Ingrid Van Den Hoogen, Sun's vice president of marketing and brand communications. "I told Scott it was an interesting concept, but we needed to probe on what made it unique in the market."[11]

McNealy's view is that technology provides far greater value than just enabling people to send and access information. Technology, he suggests, allows people around the world to participate in the world—to search for jobs, to learn, to buy and sell products, to create businesses, or to get better health care. By making it easier for people to access the Internet network, much of which is run on Sun technologies, everyone can better his or her life.

"The company did an incredible amount of soul searching," explains Karen Kahn, Sun's vice president of global communications. "We spent six months talking about the idea, figuring out how it could support our business strategy, and planning how our technologies could help organizations like Oxfam, Bono's ONE Campaign, and the United Nations. We wanted this to be a cause that everyone in the company could get behind, talk about, and be proud of. And it has become just that."[12]

Having this point of view, which Sun calls the "Participation Age," has simplified Sun's executive communications, sales conversations, media and analyst relations, and employee communications. People like to talk about the idea, according to Kahn. It's inspirational yet logical, bold yet pragmatic. The idea doesn't need to be scripted, messaged, rehearsed, and trained. It provides glue, connecting the voices of multiple Sun executives, yet letting them speak in their own voices.

How does this point of view bring to life Sun's vision of "everyone and everything participating on the network"? By sharing more—whether ideas, computer code, or technology standards—more people, especially the disadvantaged, are able to get on the network more quickly. The more people participating on the network, the bigger the market for Sun's network technologies to support all the sharing.

So, all Sun's talk about sharing adds up! Holding conferences at the United Nations about how organizations can help accelerate the rise of the Participation Age connects to the vision. Funding a Share the Opportunity global giving program to help eliminate the digital divide connects to the vision. Sharing code and resources with other technology companies connects to the vision. Creating a text-messaging program that lets U2 concert fans learn more about the Make Poverty History and ONE campaigns connects to Sun's vision. The point of view glues the tactics to the vision.

"If you ain't on the Internet, you aren't participating in the greatest accumulation of creativity on the planet ever," McNealy told *Fortune*'s David Kirkpatrick. "Look at Wikipedia, instant messaging, blogging, podcasting, home shopping, telemedicine, home banking, distance learning, voice-over IP. The problem is that three-in-four folks on the earth aren't there yet. There's a huge digital divide. Our mission is to provide the infrastructure that powers the participation age. But our cause is to eliminate the digital divide. That's personal."[13]

A Letter from Scott McNealy[14]

In the last twenty-five years, we have been living through the "Information Age," so named because of the impact information technologies have had on our lives. It's a valid label, as the commerce of information today represents a huge percentage of all economic activity in the world. Millions upon millions of people produce information, refine it, store it and distribute it; billions consume it in the same way we consume air, food, and water.

Unfortunately, though, there's one thing wrong with this world view: The Information Age is so last millennium.

Get past it!

Welcome to the "Participation Age." Advances in technology have made it possible for more and more people to connect with each other to participate and to share work flows, to compete for jobs, to purchase goods and services, to learn and create.

Information Age thinking says, "Control the creation and distribution of information and you dominate markets." Participation Age is the antithesis of all that. It's all about access. That access allows for value to be created through networked human beings who share, interact, and solve problems. Because of participation, meaningful content, connections, and relationships are created like never before.

In the Participation Age, there are no arbitrary distinctions between passengers and crew, actors and the audience. Be the one, be both, be everything in between.

Welcome to the revolution.

—Scott

Dove's Campaign for Real Beauty started with a belief that challenged assumptions

Dove's belief that there is no one single image of beauty—that it comes in all sizes and shapes—helped the company develop its much talked about Campaign for Real Beauty. Since the launch of the program, the market share for Dove's firming products grew from 7 percent to 13.5 percent in its six largest markets (United Kingdom, France, Germany, Italy, Spain, and the Netherlands).

Dove's campaign began with a point of view, based on consumer insights that beauty comes in all ages, shapes, and sizes. Beauty is not defined by youthfulness or slenderness or a flawless complexion. There is no one image of beauty.

Taking a contrarian approach to conventional beauty product marketing, Dove decided not to feed off women's insecurities about how they look or to use media images of Barbie doll–like beauty that would only make most of us women feel even worse about our bodies.

Instead, Dove decided to celebrate women's real beauty, with all our bumps and wrinkles. They changed the market conversation and stirred up talk on *Oprah, The Today Show, The New York Times Magazine,* and among women's everyday conversations. (Heck, we even talked about it at my book club.)

Dove's point of view hit a nerve. And it provided the "glue" for marketing programs. Advertising featured photographs of older women and of six everyday women clad in underwear celebrating their "real curves." Public relations released findings from a study of more than 3,200 women that Dove conducted with Harvard University and the London School of Economics to learn about women's views on their own beauty. (Only 2 percent of those women considered themselves beautiful.)

Women from the Dove ads appeared on talk shows. Dove created a special Web site encouraging debate and discussion. "When did beauty become limited by age?" they asked. "It's time to think, talk, and learn how to make beauty real again. Join Dove and the debate at campaignforbeauty.com."

"Maybe it's somehow inevitable that marketing, which caused much of the underlying anxiety (about only-thin-is-beautiful body image) in the first place, can offer up a point of view that blithely tries to resolve that anxiety," wrote Rob Walker in *The New York Times Magazine*.[15]

The point of view gives the campaign conversational value—whether you've seen the campaign or have simply heard about it. Points of view get attention and stir up talk.

Dove also created the Dove Self-Esteem Fund, which promotes itself as "an agent of change to educate and inspire girls on a wider definition of beauty. Too many girls develop low self-esteem from hang-ups about looks and, consequently, fail to reach their full potential in later life."[16]

In the United States, the Dove Self-Esteem Fund and the Girl Scouts of the USA joined together to create the "uniquely ME!" program to promote improved self-esteem among girls age 8 to 14 in the United States and Puerto Rico.

The important thing to note here is that the point of view was rooted in deep beliefs. It challenged beauty-marketing assumptions. It had substance and meaning. It was framed in engaging language and visuals. It was eminently talk-worthy and connected the marketing tactics to the brand's vision and the company's strategy.

> ## Women & Infants Hospital knows what women want—dignity, hope, belonging, and strength

You don't need to be a multibillion-dollar business to use point-of-view conversational marketing. Women & Infants Hospital, founded in 1884 in Providence, Rhode Island, as the Providence Lying-In maternity hospital, has evolved into one of the nation's leading specialty hospitals for women and newborns. The primary teaching affiliate of Brown Medical School for obstetrics, gynecology, and newborn pediatrics, Women & Infants is now the eleventh largest obstetrical service in the country with more than 9,700 deliveries annually.

In a declining market, Women & Infants continues to grow its market share. In a conversation about the hospital's success, May Kernan, the vice president of marketing communications, said:

> We're passionate about women's health and well-being, and we believe that all women should be treated with dignity. This deep-seated belief in dignity supersedes everything and guides everything we do.
>
> You can always differentiate a brand on character and beliefs. But the beliefs need to be authentic, deep in your gut. They have to be about who you're trying to serve, not about the organization. It needs to be other-oriented. And you need to bring those beliefs alive in marketing programs that develop lifelong relationships. I think we've built trust with women because we develop a bond with them through our marketing programs. We're providing advice, education, services, and doing it with dignity and a respectful sense of humor.[17]

Treating women with dignity shapes the hospital's marketing programs, the design of its hospital rooms, the extra services offered to women—like candlelit dinners for new moms and dads—and, most important, the attitude of everyone who works at the hospital, from the people who staff the registration desks to the nurses and doctors.

The belief in dignity also means that the hospital engages women and listens intently to them. In fact, last year the hospital launched "What Women Want," a program that asks women—through e-mail, newsletters, and advertising—to share their ideas about what they'd like the hospital to offer. Women are asked: "What makes you happy, what makes you feel accomplished, what brings you comfort or support, what brings you a sense of peace and wellness? What are your causes? What are your secret indulgences? E-mail us to let us know. And we'll work to bring you programs, make connections, and leverage our collective strengths to help give you what you want."[18]

The responses to the program have been overwhelming, says Kernan. "We have appealed to women to engage with us through all of our print communications, paid ads, Web site, events and classes, even suggestion boxes in the lobby. We once used the call center line as our point of contact and to measure impact. We are now using the Women & Infants' Web site. More than sixty thousand unique visitors connect with us through our site, not bad for a local hospital!"[19]

Women & Infants Hospital found three overriding patterns in what women want and what dignity means *to them*: a sense of belonging, a strong body and mind, and hope for the future.

In response to the messages it received, Women & Infants Hospital has expanded program offerings at its Centers for Health Education located throughout Rhode Island, created an annual *What Women Want* educational conference, and brought women's ideas back into the organization, helping to shape services.

The vision of Women & Infants Hospital is "to define the standard of care for women." The view of treating women with dignity, and engaging them in defining standards of care through "What Women Want," all lend support to the vision.

"You have to keep up with what women want and continually tweak marketing programs to deliver on the cause," says Kernan. "But it's easy to stay passionate when you believe in your cause."[20] This sounds basic. So why don't more companies have a point of view?

♦ *No one is in charge of creating views that help jump-start conversations.* Business is moving quickly into a world of conversations—more quickly than most marketing organizations are evolving into conversationalists. Companies are just beginning to acknowledge the need to let go of traditional one-way, command-and-control, inform-or-entertain marketing.

♦ *There are too many tactical obsessions and distractions.* A lot of the talk about "marketing as conversations" has been obsessively focused on new tools and tactics like blogs and podcasting. Although those tools have their uses, what really matters is that marketers understand what it takes to have conversations. Conversations involve listening in new ways and having something interesting and meaningful to talk about.

♦ *Too much committee mush and too many alpha fraidy cats are involved.* Many alpha fraidy cats haven't yet been indoctrinated into the talk world. They still want to control messages and produce things like ads, brochures, and other so-called content. They're uncomfortable with the dynamic world of uncovering ideas worth talking about—and setting those ideas loose, where people can talk about them in their own words and in their own style—where ideas may live or die.

Influential alpha fraidy cats claw down a true point of view as soon as it's put on the whiteboard. For this reason, senior-level executives should be involved in the process as early as possible. In addition to voicing their beliefs and perspectives, they can rule on what the company feels confident talking about and how well it helps bigger picture business objectives.

Even if the fraidy cats spend weeks and months polishing the perfectly crafted message, the message might not interest customers or get talked about by the sales reps. An idea or message may be perfect on a piece of paper, but if it's not talk-worthy, it's not a good message.

♦ *"Oops, we forgot to involve communications professionals."* Many communications people have deep insights into what makes for genuine, interesting conversations—often deeper than marketing execs. That's because the latter have been trained in traditional "telling" techniques such as advertising, direct mail, and promotions. Few have communications expertise on their staff or people with communications skills in their backgrounds. Without the voice of communications pros, they stay stuck in their old ways.

(FYI: Some of the best communications people come from political backgrounds, where developing points of view and talking with influencers is fundamental to winning and survival.)

Moving from transactional to conversational communications

Without a point of view, communications is a simple transaction. "Here's what I intend to tell you," "Here's the data to back it up," "Now I've told you," "Good-bye." It is like a financial transaction at a bank. You fill out a deposit slip, hand it to the teller, the teller hands back a receipt, you leave.

Transactional communication, like going into most banks, lets you remain detached and unengaged. It doesn't help build relationships or richer understanding.

Carly Fiorina is regarded as a superb communicator. She is smart and articulate, able to handle tough questions, and she has great stage presence. However, as CEO of Hewlett Packard, she was a transactional communicator. Her point of view for a while was that acquiring Compaq would be good for shareholders and good for customers. After the acquisition, she didn't have a point of view. Despite great communications skills, her talk often seemed empty and unstrategic. It didn't help to build confidence or trust with customers, shareholders, or her board of directors.

Did Fiorina have no beliefs about her industry that would be worth talking about? That seems unlikely. Rather, Fiorina, or her advisers, promoted her as a glamorous CEO celebrity, rather than helping her listen to the industry and talk about those views that were most relevant to customers and shareholders.

As Jim Collins, author of *Good to Great: Why Some Companies Make the Leap—and Others Don't*, explained in a *Wall Street Journal* "Manager's Journal" column, "The really striking point is that Ms. Fiorina had been in the job less than six months before she posed for the cover of *Forbes* as a superhero savior. Yet she hadn't done anything significant. And now, two years later, she still hasn't done anything significant."[21]

Or consider Time Warner CEO Dick Parsons, another intelligent, well-spoken, highly respected executive who exudes confident authority. Yet he often seems at a loss for something to talk about. When *Fortune* magazine writer Stephanie Mehta asked

Parsons about his plan for Time Warner, he responded, "It's not terribly different from what you see today. We aspire to be the best diversified media company in the world, to create and package the best content and to deliver it in more ways to more people than any other company."

"He might as well be reading from a script," wrote Mehta of the conversation.[22]

Parsons could have said something like, "Consumers spend twice as much of their personal income on entertainment as they did just five years ago. The market turmoil lies in the fact that *how* consumers want their entertainment and *how* companies have traditionally delivered it is not just a gap—it's a canyon. That's what we're working on."

Saying something like that wouldn't have given away strategy or even provided information that might be considered material by the SEC. But it's more interesting than sounding like a stiff robot with no point of view. It also pulls us into the discussion, helps us know Parsons a bit more as a person, and gives us a sense that he's perfectly aware of the immense challenges and suggests he may know how to address them.

The absence of a point of view too often leads people to think that there's a lack of strategy, understanding, or commitment, which of course isn't always the case.

In today's conversational world, business can't default to focusing exclusively on products and services. That's just not interesting to most customers. Nor is it particularly memorable or interesting to talk about.

Sun's participation belief incorporates its technology, but it's not *about* the technology. The company talks about why participating in a global technology infrastructure can end the digital divide and change the world for the better.

Women & Infants Hospital's belief in dignity transcends the services it offers to patients.

Dove's "Campaign for Beauty" doesn't talk about its firming lotions. Instead it jump-starts conversations about women's sense of beauty and self-esteem. And in doing so, it connects women with the brand.

Luther Blount doesn't talk about how great his small cruise ships are. He talks about why a real vacation should be an escape from touristy spots, and about how vacationers should spend their money on getting to their destinations, not on luxury-liner frills.

Do you agree with all these points of view? Probably not. Would you pay attention to them if you were a customer? Probably. Would talking about these ideas influence how you think and feel about the organization? Almost definitely. But would talking with these companies exclusively about their products and services be interesting? No way!

To engage people, we have to be willing to share our beliefs, perspectives, and opinions. Fortunately, these beliefs and views already exist. You don't need to hire an outrageously expensive Madison Avenue advertising firm to "create" them for you.

Chapter 4 shows you seven ways to uncover them.

Chapter 4

Listen up: Seven ways to uncover talk-worthy ideas

"The secret is to reach deep into your soul to talk about what you believe in, as it affects your audience," I told a marketing director in explaining how to find a point of view.

"That may be true, but how do we do *that?* When we think about what we believe in, we default to things like increasing margins and revenue, producing quality products that provide value to our customers. That doesn't sound interesting or new," shot back the marketing director.

Okay. Let's break it down. The following seven ways can help you uncover fresh ideas to talk about, ideas that can help people get to know organizations in a deeper way:

1. Tap into the CEO's beliefs
2. Listen in new ways
3. Run a point-of-view workshop (but never on a Monday)
4. Hold a clarity council

5. Think more narrowly
6. Explore new metaphors
7. Go on a walkabout

Tap into the CEO's beliefs

CEOs spend most of their day talking with customers, analysts, investors, employees, and partners about ideas, trends, issues, and problems. Executives take CEO positions, which are all-encompassing, because of their passion for the company and what's possible. They live the business. They're driven by their beliefs.

"First and the most important is that you have to know what you believe if you want to be a leader," said Rudy Giuliani in a commencement speech to Middlebury College in May 2005. "You have to have strong beliefs. You have to know what you stand for. You can't lead other people unless you know what you stand for. You have to spend a great deal of your time trying to figure that out and trying to determine what's important to you, what goals you want to achieve."[1]

Giuliani suggests that leaders have strong beliefs. So how do we extract those from our CEOs? One way is by annually asking the following twelve "What We Believe Questions." Set aside two hours and tape the conversation so that you capture the language, tone, and sentiment. As you talk about the questions with the CEO, keep asking him or her, "Why should customers (or employees or stockholders) care about this? What's the value *to them* of knowing this?" This focus on what the ideas mean to others will help make sure that the CEO's ideas aren't all about your company and products.

1. We believe passionately that . . .
2. People in our industry are wasting too much time talking about . . .
3. The thing that our customers should be worrying about is . . .
4. Conventional thinking says (fill in the blank about a relevant industry issue), but the real issue is . . .
5. Solving this one problem would change the game for our customers . . .
6. We never want to be associated with . . .
7. Our product category matters more/less today because . . .
8. People think the problem is . . . , but it's really . . .
9. What I'd really like to say to prospects is . . .
10. To make customers believers, they need to understand this one thing . . .
11. If I had a crystal ball, I'd predict these three changes for our industry over the next two years . . .
12. What gets me most excited about (our industry/our business) is . . .

Another approach, one used by Intuit CEO Steve Bennett to get ideas out of founder Scott Cook's brain, is to ask executives to boil down ideas into coherent repeatable phrases as Scott Mc-Nealy did at Sun with "sharing and participating," or a single word as May Kernan did at Women & Infants with "dignity."

One of Cook's phrases is "savoring the surprises." It's a perspective—a point of view—on the business. Cook uses the phrase throughout the company. It's a perspective that guides how Intuit gets inside customers' heads to look for new product ideas.[2]

These phrases aren't meant to be tag lines. They're simply

shorthand for beliefs that people understand, repeat, and develop successful programs around.

Listen in new ways

Listening, in many ways, is marketing.

In a conversational marketing world, listening becomes the communications star and talking takes on a lesser role. After all, in a meaningful conversation we aren't always talking, but we *are* always listening.

I don't mean listening as a prelude to figuring out how to market to people. And I don't mean listening as a finale, for measuring programs after the fact. I mean listening in an ongoing, active way.

Who other than marketing is responsible for uncovering insights and bringing them into the company? Who other than marketing to see things from the customer's point of view—and advocate for the customer with product management, customer service, and business strategy?

Listening carefully provides clues to what people are talking about, what they're concerned and frustrated about, what trends are dissipating or emerging, what language and feelings resonate with customers. An added benefit is that when people feel you're listening, they trust you more. And the more they trust you, the more they'll tell you how to give them what they want.

Listening is open-ended. The purpose is not necessarily to confirm our hypotheses or to get answers. It's about tuning in to what *other* people want to talk about, taking a real interest in what they have to say. It shakes our assumptions and shifts our perspective. It helps us understand where the other person is coming from. It helps us see his or her point of view.

"Through listening to others carefully, we are able to step imaginatively and empathetically into their shoes, and to experience the world from an entirely different point of view," write Jaida N'Ha Sandra and Jon Spayde in *Salons: The Joy of Conversations.*[3] The authors, former writers for *Utne Reader* magazine and longtime "salon keepers," advocate for listening "in between the lines as someone speaks, hearing the feelings and the intentions as well as the words. It requires tremendous discipline."

Listen for emotion

When Republicans in Congress began talking about eliminating the two-hundred-year-old senatorial filibuster, they felt fairly confident in their ability to succeed. The Democrats were deeply troubled, believing that without the filibuster, Republicans could quickly get their Supreme Court justice nominations approved.

The GOP is quite skilled at listening and understanding how to shape points of view that are relevant and emotionally appealing. So, when the Republicans began to mount a campaign to eliminate the filibuster, Democrats listened—really listened—to try to find a way to counter the Republicans.

Democratic researcher Geoff Garin didn't so much lead focus groups as listen to them for clues and emotional triggers. He heard people talk about the "arrogance" of Republicans and their fears about "abuse of power."

Hearing about these fears especially struck Garin. (Remember how important emotion is to meaning making?) "Abuse of power" provided a point of view for the Democrats' discussions. It was powerful, simple, and easy to talk about. It was a clear, repeatable phrase: *abuse of power.* Easy for Democrats to remember and use in their own words and in their own style, which they did.

"During an appearance on 'This Week with George Stephanopoulos,' Senator Charles Schumer of New York needed all of thirty seconds to evoke the 'abuse of power' theme— twice," according to *The New York Times Magazine*. "By the time Senator Reid took to the airwaves . . . ('This abuse of power is not what our founders intended,' he told the camera solemnly), the issue seemed pretty well defined in the public mind."[4]

The Republicans backed down. The filibuster remains.

Why we don't listen

So why don't we listen more? Well, for one thing our business culture views listening as unproductive and not serious business. We're not "making" anything concrete, tangible, and measurable from the act of listening. Few of us get raises or better performance ratings for listening.

There's also the rush to solve the problem, which is an especially difficult challenge for us Type A's. As Daniel Yankelovich explains in *The Magic of Dialogue*, "In a typical discussion, almost as soon as the problem surfaces, someone is bound to say, 'Well, what are we going to do about it?' End of dialogue about problem; beginning of a rush of ideas for leaping into the fray and doing something . . . as long as it smacks of action."[5] Plus, most of us were never trained to listen. It's a new discipline.

Jiddu Krishnamurti, the Indian philosopher, once explained in his *Talks and Dialogues* why it's so difficult to listen:

> I do not know if you have ever examined how you listen, it doesn't matter to what, whether to a bird, to the wind in the leaves, to the rushing waters, or how you listen in a dialogue with yourself, to your conversation in various relationships with your intimate friends, your wife or husband. If we try to listen we find it extraordinarily difficult, because

we are always projecting our opinions and ideas, our prej-
udices, our background, our inclinations, our impulses;
when they dominate, we hardly listen at all to what is being said. In that state there is no value at all. One listens,
and therefore learns, only in a state of attention, a state of
silence, in which this whole background is in abeyance, is
quiet; then, it seems to me, it is possible to communicate.[6]

Listening means putting our own points of view aside and
intently focusing on what others are saying, why they're saying
it, and how they're saying it with their words, metaphors, and
stories.

Passive-listening tools

One way to listen passively to market whisperings and emerging
trends is to monitor blogs for what is being talked about in the
industry and about issues, products, and the company. As I write
this book, there are fifty-eight million blogs in the Blogosphere,
and approximately seventy-five thousand new ones are launched
each day. Some have valuable, honest opinions; others are
merely rants from the terminally disgruntled. But by analyzing
the whole Blogosphere, marketers can see valuable patterns,
thereby pinpointing emerging trends and highlighting customer
dissatisfaction.

Software tools from companies like Cymfony, Biz 360, Um-
bria, and Nielsen/Buzz Metrics send an application called a spi-
der over the Web to track postings about their clients, classifying
the postings by topics, geography, organization, and person,
and even identifying the sentiment of opinion by using language parsing software. In other words, these tools can classify
whether the bloggers' sentiments on a particular topic are positive or negative.

A free tool to track aggregated blog opinions is Nielsen/ BuzzMetrics's BlogPulse site. Type in a topic or company name, specify the time period you're tracking, and up comes a chart plotting the level of activity and allowing you to click on any point in the chart to read the blog postings for that point. BlogPulse also offers a free Trend Search, which allows you to map graphs that visually track aggregated blog conversations for discrete topics.

Figure 4-1 shows one that maps the conversations on cancer, heart disease, and strokes over a six-month period.

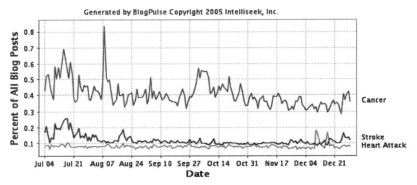

Figure 4-1. BlogPulse™, a service of Nielsen/BuzzMetrics.

One of the interesting things about the chart in Figure 4-1 is that it shows much more blog chatter about cancer and even strokes than heart attacks, even though heart disease is the leading cause of death. It shows there is an opportunity for hospitals with a cardiology specialty, or pharmaceutical companies with new cardio drugs, or even the American Heart Association to improve the market conversation so there is more talk about the disease that is more likely to kill people.

Another helpful tool is NetroCity's visual search service that goes beyond blogs and beyond simply classifying conversations by topics.

NetroCity pulls in every digital item—blogs, forums, and news—and visually maps patterns and relationships among topics. It paints graphical patterns synthesized from hundreds to tens of thousands of news items, helping us to see overarching patterns in an industry or around an issue.

The tool helps show what topics or companies—or what topics *and* companies—in an industry are being talked about the most, which are "connected" and being discussed in the same context and which are increasing in "volume" or dissipating.

NetroCity's visual search maps provide patterns that let us see how others view our company, which is sometimes a different picture than how we see our company's position. These maps help answers questions such as the following:

* What are the most popular conversation topics in a particular industry, or around a particular topic?
* What companies are most closely connected to these topics?
* What issues is the company connected with, according to news and blog conversations?
* Which of our competitors do people lump in with us when they talk about the industry?
* How close to the center of the market discussion is the company—or how far?
* Which topics are so peripheral that they don't deserve any marketing attention?

The NetroCity map in Figure 4-2 shows the most popular and connected topics around retirement and financial planning for a three-month period. The larger the square and the closer to the center of the axis, the more conversation about the topic. Ideas talked about within the same contexts are closer together and linked by thicker lines.

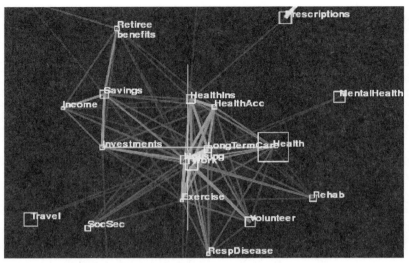

Figure 4-2. NetroCity Event Radar™.

If I were marketing health insurance, I'd look closely at the topics closely connected to health insurance—long-term care, rehab services, and health accounts—and create points of view on those topics. If I were a real estate developer targeting older people, I'd talk about nearby opportunities to continue working and to volunteer because "work" and "volunteering" are closely connected to housing on this map. I'd also talk about exercise, a third topic close to housing.

These NetroCity maps give marketers a clearer direction about where to focus their market conversations, as well as clues about how to connect their point of view with other contextually relevant topics.

How to listen more actively: Communities and listening tours

Although viewing aggregated data is useful for quickly getting the lay of the land in trends and consumer opinions, online communities and forums also provide insights, as does getting out into the real world and doing listening tours.

Online communities are sites for people with similar interests to get together, to share ideas, and to talk about trends, products, and companies. Companies sponsor some of these communities. Other groups are people with common interests creating an online space to talk and share ideas.

All provide fascinating clues about what people are talking about—what they like, what they think is cool or stupid, what they do and don't want from companies, what trends they're especially tuned into.

A lot goes on at NikeTalk, an online community for people interested in talking about sneakers, but it isn't affiliated with Nike. Millions of site visitors talk about their opinions on different sneaker brands, types of sneakers, sports, and music; they even share their "sneaker art." For anyone in the footwear industry, conversations on these sites are quite interesting.

Another self-organizing community is TiVoCommunity.com. The 125,000 members of this community share ideas on how to get the most out of all TiVo's features, how to create complementary applications, how be a better "TiVotee," and even how to convince friends to buy a TiVo.

Communispace, a Boston-based company, manages more than 250 private communities for companies like Hallmark, Starwood Hotels, Unilever, and Charles Schwab. Because these communities are private, members contribute much more than people do on public online forums, according to Communispace executives.

"Communities help companies shut up and really listen to their customers," Communispace CEO Diane Hessan told me. "The insights from these communities are extraordinary. Sometimes I can't believe just how honest and forthcoming people are with one another and with the companies. If you really listen to customers, you'll not only find interesting things to talk about, you'll find ideas on how to grow your business."[7]

Hallmark community members provided real-life anecdotes that helped successfully revamp the greeting card company's line of Shoebox greeting cards. Charles Schwab CEO Chuck Schwab asked 400 high net worth members of Schwab's private online community for information about their investing strategies and market advice before he went out on a market tour. "He [Schwab] had the highest response to date from our community members," said Jonathan Craig, a Schwab vice president responsible for marketing services to Schwab's affluent independent investors. "Clients were literally writing essays to him about what they liked and what needed improvement."[8]

Alison Zelen, director of consumer and market insights for Unilever's deodorant category in North America, told people at a 2005 American Marketing Association conference that she started a community for young guys so that she and her team could really get inside the heads of their target customers. She explained:

> Trust me, it's really hard not to sound like their parents, the typical company trying to sell them something, or like you're trying way too hard to be cool. Our community not only helps us learn about strategically relevant brand issues, it also helps us get into their heads and understand what makes them tick. Because the AXE guys talk to one another as well as us, we can observe them talking as if they were in the locker room. So we aren't influencing their word choice or the tone of their language. It's really great for us marketers, who are anywhere from two to fifteen years older than our target, to hear what they talk about.[9]

Unilever uses what it learns from the community for developing new products, messaging, and point-of-view creative concepts.

Get out on a listening tour

Listening tours are nothing more than stepping out into the market with an open mind and talking with customers, or employees, or, in the case of political candidates, voters. It's a way to hear what's on people's minds and to see patterns of what's important to people, and why.

Effective listening tours aren't usually delegated to junior people using formulaic questionnaires. It's not a "getting answers" tour; it's a "taking-the-pulse-listening-and-conversation" tour. The more you listen, the more you learn.

When Gary Kusin began as CEO at Kinko's, he spent his first six months visiting all 200 Kinko stores in the United States and meeting with more than 2,500 employees. "The most important thing I heard was that our customers have changed. They don't just need a quick turnaround copy job in the middle of the night. They want to know that they can partner with us for bigger jobs," he explained.[10]

A few years ago I went on a listening tour of SAP, the third largest software company in the world, along with Steve Mann, the company's vice president of competitive intelligence. Our objective was to talk with new customers to learn about their experience during the sales process. We wanted to better understand the following issues:

* What information had been helpful?
* What would they have liked to understand better?
* What did they just not care much about?

We found that prospects wanted less information about SAP's products and technology and more insights about industry trends and what those trends might mean to *their* businesses.

"We don't want to hear all about your products; we can have people on our staff look that information up on the Web," customers told us. "We want to talk to SAP about their insights into our industry. SAP works with all the major players in our industry and has a better view than we do of the big picture trends that are emerging and how companies are addressing them. Talk to us about 'next practices,' not just 'best practices.'"[11]

As a result of the listening tour, SAP began refocusing its marketing conversations to talk more about industry insights and future trends, and, as an added benefit, slashed the amount of sales collateral it produced because customers said they just didn't find sales collateral valuable.

During listening tours ask people about themselves, about what they like and don't like, about what they value and don't value. Listening tours engage people in conversations about both rational and emotional concerns that are relevant to your mutual interests. One of the secrets to a successful listening tour is asking good questions.

The World Café Community, which has established a process for bringing people together to talk about ideas and to collectively solve problems, believes that "good questions—ones that we care about and want to answer—call us outward to one another. They are an invitation to explore, to venture out, to risk, to listen, to abandon our positions. Good questions help us become both curious and uncertain and this is always the road that opens us to the surprise of new insight."[12]

Knowing that questions are critical to conversations, the World Café Community offers the following suggestions:[13]

* Well-crafted questions attract energy and focus our attention on what really counts. Pose open-ended questions.
* Good questions need not imply immediate action steps or problem solving. They should invite inquiry and discovery versus advocacy and advantage.
* You'll know you have a good question when it continues to surface new ideas and possibilities.
* Good questions sustain interest and energy.

After asking good questions, listen to what the answers tell about people's ideas, wants, needs, likes and dislikes, language, and sentiment.

Here's an example of some listening tour questions that the National Assembly of State Arts Association used in talking with Montana's political leaders to try to better understand the context and climate for the arts:

* What do you value most about living in Montana?
* How would you describe the character of your communities?
* What's the biggest threat or concern you have for your town?
* What would be your example of a successful citizen of your town?
* What brought you to public service?
* What led you to choose your political party?
* When you're faced with more worthy causes than money, how do set your priorities?
* Do you remember an arts experience that made an impression on you?

Active listening: Making people feel "listened to"
Some of the best listeners are broadcast journalists, whose careers depend on being good listeners. I asked Robin Young, cohost of

the public radio program *Here & Now* and former *Today* show guest host, about what five things make for an interesting conversation. Her reply included the following tips:

1. Listening.
2. Really, listening.
3. After you've listened, asking questions relative to what you heard when you listened.
4. Then, listen to the answer.
5. And . . . follow up with another question, to make sure you heard correctly what the speaker was saying.
5a. Then . . . listen some more.

To build trust with people—trust that is necessary for them to tell us how to give them what they want—we have to make them feel *listened to*. This is important in face-to-face conversations, in online communities, and through marketing and sales programs. However, asking for opinions but never acknowledging those opinions is not real listening. It's just another form of conventional market research, designed to help the company but not build a relationship with the customer. Real listening gleans ideas and builds relationships.

Dr. Walter Carl, assistant professor of communications at Northeastern University, explained to me that there are three general categories of listening, a sort of Maslow's hierarchy of listening if you will. People tend to feel "listened to" when they reach the "endorsement" level:

1. *Recognition*—simply recognizing the other person's existence
2. *Acknowledgment*—acknowledging what another person feels or thinks or says (paraphrasing is often used to do this)

3. *Endorsement*—accepting another person's thoughts or point of view as valid and legitimate

Here's how this listening hierarchy works for talking with customers through channels like customer communities, managing a customer service organization, or in word-of-mouth marketing campaigns.

Providing an easy way for customers to provide ideas or even to complain is a way of showing recognition. Providing a relevant response that shows that the company hears and appreciates the idea or complaint demonstrates acknowledgment. (Note: you have to listen to the tone and emotion of the comment to provide a relevant response.)

The endorsement level requires more than most companies are willing to give. It involves having a conversation or dialogue with customers so that the marketers get the full context of where the customers are coming from and what's interesting to them. Endorsement doesn't imply that the company agrees with the customers' points of view, just that it recognizes and respects the validity and legitimacy of their beliefs.

If a company can't or chooses not to act on the customer's suggestion or complaint, then it's important to explain why the organization isn't able to make changes or a why the changes aren't feasible. By taking time to have the conversation, the company shows that it understands and appreciates the validity of the customer's comments but that the company also has a legitimate position. Few companies, according to Carl, ever reach the endorsement stage, which is too bad because it is only at this level that loyal relationships develop, many of which lead to customers becoming advocates for the company—even customers who had once complained.

Several academic studies have found that companies that respond to customer complaints or negative comments at the endorsement level—accepting the customer's response as valid and engaging in a respectful dialogue—can deter these customers from passing along negative word-of-mouth and even turn dissatisfied customers into loyal ones. According to a study published in *The Journal of Retailing:*

> As long as the retailer ensures satisfaction, most complainants will not engage in negative word of mouth or exit. Rather, because they perceive the retailer as being fair and just, these complainants may actually become more loyal customers.[14]

The authors note that it's important for companies to genuinely acknowledge the customer's complaint, going so far as thanking the customer for raising the problem, and then reassuring the customer that the retailer is committed to improving.

Companies that fear losing control, or fear having customers post negative reviews about their products, have nothing to fear—if they are sincerely interested in those customers' views and are willing to acknowledge, recognize, and endorse the customers' opinions as valid and legitimate. Complaining is a conversation that doesn't need to turn negative if each party respects the other's point of view and communicates honestly about the issues. But woe to companies that don't embrace this Maslow-like hierarchy of listening in our new conversational world. That's when negative word-of-mouth can spread like wildfire.

What to listen for

There are three important things to listen for: intent, content, and language.

Intent helps us understand the emotion, feeling, and sentiment behind the words. Is the person excited and passionate about what he or she is saying? Is the person frustrated? Does the person find it ludicrous? Or, perhaps the person just feels that it's matter of fact, no big deal one way or the other.

The tone is a clue to what the person feels about what is being said. (As noted previously, social psychologists have found that people can accurately judge the attitudes and intentions of other people from a few dozen seconds observing tone of voice, body gesture, and language.) *How* things are said speaks volumes.

Content helps us understand the facts and information. One way to listen is to listen as if you'll have to later explain the information to someone else. Another way is paraphrasing what's being said to make sure you're hearing it correctly.

The third thing to listen for is lexicon and language. Studies have proven that people advocate for companies and for people with whom they identify. The more customers feel that they identify or relate to those in your company—or to your company's customers—the greater the likelihood that those customers will become loyal advocates.

Identity triggers advocacy significantly more than trust or customer satisfaction, according to a recent University of Queensland study.[15] In fact, being satisfied with the product or service accounted for only 21 percent of the study participants becoming advocates, while identification accounted for 62 percent of the participants becoming advocates. "Consumer identification exists when a consumer feels a connection to a company and feels like he or she is part of a community of like-minded customers," said the authors of the study.

To help customers bond and identify, marketers can do the following:

* Make it easy for customers to get to know like-minded customers by opening an online community for customers where they can talk with their peers.
* Hold informal customer salons where customers have an opportunity to talk and get to know one another.
* Express the company's point of view and use language that is relevant to customers, helping them relate to the company. For example, if you're marketing a product to college students and you want to say that something is great or outstanding, you'd connect better with them by saying that the product was "off the hinges." Now use that same expression with a baby boomer and he'll think the product was faulty or broken.

Lexicon matters, and it's constantly shifting and changing, so marketers need to listen closely, especially if we are not similar to our customers.

On how to listen

Michael Ende describes in his book *Momo* a little girl with an exceptional ability to listen:

Little Momo could listen in a way that nobody else could. That's nothing unusual, some might say, everybody can listen.

This is not true. There are only a very few people who can really listen. And the way in which Momo listened was absolutely unique.

Momo could listen so that inarticulate folk suddenly came out with bright ideas. It wasn't anything that she said or asked that brought such ideas out of the other person; no, it wasn't that. She simply sat there and listened with full concentration, completely involved. While she gazed at them with her huge dark eyes, others felt unique ideas (which they had never guessed were there) suddenly surfacing from deep within.

She could listen so well that restless or undecided people suddenly realized exactly what they wanted. The timid unexpectedly felt free and bold. Those who felt unlucky or depressed exuded confidence and joy. And if somebody felt that something was missing from his life, which had become meaningless (that he was only one of the teeming masses; that he could not manage and would be discarded like a broken jar)—then he would go and tell little Momo all about it. While he spoke about it, it would become clear in some secret hidden way, that he was basically mistaken; that there was only one of him, that he was unique and because of that, he was important to the world.

How Momo could listen![16]

Run a point-of-view workshop (but never on Monday)

Another way to find interesting ideas to talk about is to bring together people in the company to brainstorm ideas in a point-of-view workshop. Workshops can generate many potential conversational themes or they can bomb, torturing everyone involved and scaring people away from the notion that all companies have ideas worth talking about. Here's how to run a fun, productive workshop.

First, never hold a workshop on a Monday, maybe not even on a Tuesday. From many years of experience, I've found that it's difficult to engage people at the beginning of the week. Monday is for catching up on e-mail, planning the rest of the week, and getting your head back in the game. Thursdays are the best days, with Wednesday coming in a close second. (By noon on Friday, people are itchy to get out of the work mode and don't fully concentrate.)

Set aside a full day and start early. Get a good recording device to capture the group discussions. You want to be able to capture the sentiment, tone, and emotion as well as the content of what's said. Having someone take notes won't capture the tone and emotion.

Invite up to twenty people to participate. Ideally invite the CEO, particularly if you haven't discussed the twelve "What We Believe" questions. Involving CEOs helps you get into interesting, compelling points of view quickly. CEOs have many well-ground beliefs about the company and usually some strong views about the industry. Plus, the organization is more likely to rally behind ideas that the CEO is talking about.

Who to invite has less to do with individuals' titles or organizational responsibilities and more to do with their qualities. A cross section of people with different experiences and perspectives is ideal. Look for people who have the following traits:

* Knowledgeable about the company, customers, and industry
* Intellectually curious
* Open-minded
* Comfortable with ambiguity and talking about possibilities and concepts
* Passionate but not zealots

* Respectful of other people's views and opinions
* Able to put aside their personal agendas for a day

Avoid including the naysayers and alpha fraidy cats—you know, those domineering people who are persuasive, smart, and articulate but are risk-averse. They naturally begin to pick an idea apart before allowing it time to breathe. Some of an organization's best process and execution mavens may in fact be the worst people to invite to a creative workshop!

Also, try to go to an interesting, relaxed place off-site instead of hunkering down in the usual conference room. A change of place helps everyone tune into the day and tune out the distractions of the office. I like places with windows and at least two walls where you can post sticky notes or clip chart pages.

Set up small café tables throughout the room. The small tables make the conversations among the groups more intimate and productive. On each table, place approximately fifteen sticky note pads, paper for doodling (some people think on paper by drawing versus writing), pens, and one flip chart at each table.

The facilitator also needs a whistle, a flip chart easel, and three pads of easel paper—preferably the kind that has the same adhesive built into it as the sticky notes (it will be easier to hang the flip chart paper on walls later in the day).

It's especially important to have a facilitator good at provoking discussion, questioning the group's assumptions, offering up contrarian perspectives about trends in your industry, guiding, and summarizing. Because these workshops are more like intellectual food fights than polite meetings, the facilitator needs to be more like a demanding, questioning university teacher than a schoolyard monitor.

Format of the workshop

I. Purpose (15 minutes)

Begin by explaining the purpose of the workshop—what you're trying to accomplish and why it matters. Examples from successful workshops include:

* "Despite a solid marketing strategy and new branding, people don't understand that we've changed our business. We need to find new ways to help people quickly understand our business strategy and why it matters to them."
* "To be perceived as a player in our market, we need to be a bigger part of the market conversations. The more interesting our industry perspectives, the easier it will be for us to get meetings with more senior-level decision makers, get analyst mind share, and get quoted by the press. Today we need to examine our beliefs and perspectives about the industry in a new way."
* "We need to find ways to get our strategy off the page so that it's much more interesting for our sales reps to discuss with customers."
* "We see the opportunities in being known as a business innovation consulting firm. What part of innovation do we want to own? What is our point of view?"
* "Our marketing communications are in a rut. Today's session is to brainstorm ideas that can bring our brand to life, helping us and everyone in the company to talk about the company in more interesting ways."

II. Introductions (15 minutes)

Next, ask each person to introduce him- or herself and briefly explain why he or she wanted to contribute to this session.

(Note: the word *contribute* suggests action and responsibility to the group members; *participate* is too passive.)

III. Warm up the group by talking about market trends and context (1.5 hours)

This part of the workshop warms people up and gets them thinking about what's happening in the business and their organization. I suggest using four to five questions for this part of the workshop. The questions should start people thinking slowly and build up in energy and style. By the end of this warm-up, people should be feeling comfortable enough to venture away from "facts" and more freely share ideas and beliefs. Some examples include the following:

* "What are our most common and significant communications obstacles? With customers, sales reps, financial analysts, employees, or media?"
* "What market trends are most—and least—important to customers?"
* "If a customer were talking to a peer about us, what would he or she say?"
* "What are we not, never want to become, and never want to be associated with?"
* "What's the one thing we would like customers to understand but they don't?"

IV. Small group 100-mile-per-hour[17] "Twelve Beliefs" session (1.5–2 hours)

In this part of the workshop you break out into small groups of four people. Each group brainstorms answers to the twelve "What We Believe In" questions. (And remember to keep reminding participants to think about these questions from the customers' point of view. Their tendency will be talk about the company's sales and marketing messages. Keep them "other" focused.)

"What We Believe In" Questions

1. We believe passionately that . . .
2. People in our industry are wasting too much time talking about . . .
3. The thing that our customers should be worrying about is . . .
4. Conventional thinking says (fill in the blank about a relevant industry issue), but the real issue is . . .
5. Solving this one problem would change the game . . .
6. We never want to be associated with . . .
7. Our product category matters more/less today because . . .
8. People think the problem is (blank), but it's really . . .
9. What I'd really like to say to prospects is . . .
10. To make customers believers, we need them to understand this one thing . . .
11. If I had a crystal ball, I'd predict these three changes for our industry over the next two years . . .
12. What gets me most excited about (our industry/our business) is . . .

Assign three questions to each group. Allow each group fifteen minutes to brainstorm ten ideas for their three questions, writing their shorthand answers on sticky notes and sticking them on the wall. At the end of fifteen minutes, the facilitator calls time or blows a whistle to end the idea session. Each group should have at least thirty ideas. The facilitator then asks the groups to edit their ideas—narrowing them down to the three they like best for each question.

Repeat this format three more times for the second, third, and fourth groups of the twelve "What We Believe In" questions.

Then take a break.

V. Highlights: What We Believe (30 minutes to 1.5 hours, depending on size of group)

When you come back from the break, go through each question, asking a representative from each breakout group to share the group's top three ideas to that question. The facilitator should write the ideas to each question on one flip chart page and then put the page up on the wall.

VI. Wrap Up: What's the One Word or Phrase?

By this time, people will be getting tired. Here's how to wrap up the session. Ask the group, "If you had to leave now and go have a conversation with a customer or *Fortune* writer about one idea, which idea would it be? Write down that word or a short phrase."

Then, ask each person to share this one word or phrase idea and why he or she likes it.

Applaud the hard work of the group.

Wrap up by telling them that you'll send a summary of the meeting within a week and will keep them in the loop on the point-of-view development process.

Hold a clearness committee

Are our perspectives engaging people or boring them? Is there something brewing in the market that we should be talking about?

It's hard to keep a fresh perspective on ideas that are worth talking about. After a while, we—and even our trusted agencies—become immune to stepping back and assessing which ideas are working and which aren't. That's why adapting the Quaker practice of Clearness Committees can help.

The purpose of the Clearness Committee is to help a congregation member assess a difficult or confusing situation. Prior to the meeting, the person seeking clarity writes a brief summary about the issue he or she is seeking clarity on and sends it to the five people invited to be members of the committee. At the meeting, the person seeking clarity briefly presents the problem or obstacle and then the committee members ask questions that help the person see the situation in a different light.

"The rules are so simple, they're radical," writes Gregg Levoy in *Callings: Finding and Following an Authentic Life*. "The advisors ask questions only. No advice, no storytelling, no windy narratives."[18] In other words, committee members are there to help, to clarify, to listen without judgment or bias—and to ask honest, caring, challenging, and open questions.

Holding a similar type of meeting once or twice a year can also clarify marketing views. It costs little, except perhaps for paying expenses and a small honorarium to the committee members. The insights are almost always helpful. Questions can be broad, or more specific to a gnawing problem that you're having, such as the following examples:

* "Sales reps say customers only want to talk price. How can we involve customers in discussions around value instead of price?"
* "We believe people in our industry need to be talking more about (issues/trend). But we can't get anyone interested in the idea. Why?"

* "How do we shift our marketing mind-set from talking all about our products to talking about broader industry issues?"
* "We're pigeonholed in this niche. How can we make our firm more relevant within the context of broader industry needs?"

Unlike an advisory council, the purpose of the marketing clarity committee is quite specific around an issue or obstacle that is impeding your success. It's a small group—no more than five people and you. This isn't a focus group where you invite your staff to sit in. To evoke advice, it must be between you and the committee members. (Although taping the session to help you replay the ideas is a good idea.)

Invite people with diverse perspectives, some who know your business and industry and others who are savvy business or communications professionals. All must be people who can be trusted to ask insightful questions, respect the confidential nature of the discussions, and are known to be superb communicators. Some types of people to consider include:

* A savvy customer (or two) who wants to help the company
* A top-performing sales rep
* A recently retired executive from your company or a competitor
* A respected editor of an industry publication
* A journalism professor, who was once a practicing business writer
* A respected communications or marketing executive, perhaps from another industry, or an experienced marketing/communications consultant with no ongoing relationship with the company

Prior to the meeting, write up a two-page brief on what you are trying to better understand or clarify, and distribute it to the committee members. Include why you want to figure out this problem, relevant background and context, and your hypothesis or hunches as to causes. (The discipline of writing this document will in itself help you see the situation in a new way.) Also, send guidelines about the meeting ahead of time so the committee members understand what's unique about the approach.

* The meeting opens with you providing a brief summary of the question or concern.
* Committee members' questions should be brief and to the point, focused on seeking answers to the question at hand. The focus is on the questions, not on lecturing or dictating advice.
* All questions, even those that seem highly intuitive or headed toward left field, are okay. They may provide new insights around the question.

Meetings should last no longer than two hours. After that time, interest and ideas begin to wilt.

Guidelines for Clearness Committees

❏ Do not spend too much time trying to clarify the history of the situation. Focus on the way forward.
❏ Keep your attention on the focus person. Sharing your own experiences, even in question form, will be a distraction.

❑ Keep your questions simple and nondirective.
❑ Do not be afraid to ask questions that seem far-fetched or even irrelevant. If they rise up in you, they probably need to be asked.
❑ Do not enter into the process feeling that you know the answer.
❑ Expect to be transformed.

Source: "A Quaker Toolbox: Guidelines for Clearness Committees," Friends General Conferences.

Think more narrowly

Another way to find a point of view is to talk about a narrower piece of a broad topic or trend. Too many companies tend to think that being "thought leaders" means talking about everything that's going on in their industry. When we focus on a narrow slice, we often provide deeper, more insightful advice that helps customers think about and talk about troubling obstacles or the one thing that they really want.

Going narrow doesn't imply that we don't understand *all* the issues, but that we understand the issues and customer needs so well that we're able to hone in on a particularly troubling aspect or an especially overlooked area that holds opportunities.

Since most people try go wide and talk about all the issues or benefits, going narrow will set you apart.

For example:

Broad topic	Narrow point of view
Fighting childhood obesity	Rethinking neighborhood playgrounds
Retirement financial planning	Planning for early debt retirement
Business innovation	Fixing the front end of innovation by inviting customers into the process
Digital marketing	Search engine advertising
Compliance	Integrity

Explore new metaphors—pigs, flying barns, and fairy tales

Metaphors help us make sense of ideas and *think* about concepts and points of view in ways that language alone cannot. Using *new* metaphors helps open up new ways of thinking and often provides new ways to express those views.

"Metaphor is typically viewed as characteristic of language alone, a matter of words rather than thought or action," explains George Lakoff and Mark Johnson in *Metaphors We Live By*.[19] "Most people think they can get along perfectly well without metaphor. We have found, on the contrary, that metaphor is pervasive in everyday life. . . . Our ordinary conceptual system is fundamentally metaphorical in nature."

In other words, by equating one thing to another, we're able to explore and see new ideas and meanings.

"Metaphors help people understand your vision and what makes a project different on so many levels," award-winning architect Chuck Dietsche told me. "Using metaphors helps me to tap into the spiritual, emotional, and mystical and put it together for people in new ways. For example, I like using the metaphor of fairy tales, with house as a place of safety and warmth, contrasting with the wild nature just outside the door."

Using a fairy tale metaphor, here's how Dietsche explains his house design called Rapunzel: "Standing sentinel beside its fraternal twin, the aptly named Rapunzel creates a childlike longing to climb to the top and let loose your imagination."

Or, in explaining the difference between designing a primary residence and a second home, Dietsche says, "The first house is a dictionary. The second is a poem." In other words, our primary homes are about accommodation: "Where do I park, where do I sleep?" While the second home idealizes our lives and helps us express that to the world.[20]

Here are a few other examples of using metaphors to think in new ways and engage people in interesting discussions.

The executive of a financial services company expressed the company's approach to talent by relating, "During an interview I ask potential employees whether they are equities or bonds, to help me understand who they really are and how they are likely to fit our needs. 'Equity' employees are more aggressive and drive new ideas and growth, while 'bond' employees are the Steady Eddies who make sure that the core business functions run day in and day out. Just like a financial portfolio, you need a mix of equities and bonds in your employees."

Management consultant Alan Weiss uses the following metaphor to help clients see the need for focus: "What we need here is an arrow, not a flying barn." This metaphor creates an immediate recognition of the need to streamline and gain aerodynamic efficiency, which is easier to deal with than pointing out that we're trying to tackle too much, we have no focus, we need to set priorities, and yada-yada-yada.

Back in the 1990s, Ford Motor Company managers used a swimming pool visual metaphor to help describe how the company's culture was changing. Then CEO Jack Nasser explained to Suzy Wetlander, then editor of *Harvard Business Review,* that employees created two videos depicting the old and the new Ford. In the old, someone falls into a pool and starts drowning while the people standing around the pool watch but do nothing. "All the people on the side of the pool start to wring their hands . . . 'God, we've got a problem. . . . Maybe we should put a committee together.' And the guy in the pool, of course, drowns. In the video depicting the new Ford, the guy falls into the pool, and everyone jumps in to save him."[21]

To explain the problems with so much cost cutting in the airline industry, Gordon Bethune, former chief executive officer of Continental Airlines, often says, "If you are being rewarded for finding ways to make pizza cheaper, you eventually take the cheese off. You make it so cheap that people won't eat it."[22]

Some metaphors have been so overused—think war and sports—that they're not helpful for thinking and engaging people in new ideas. But our culture is rich in metaphors that do help grab our imaginations.

In support of the *Harvard Business Review* article "No More Metaphors," as author Anne Miller wrote, "Selling anything today—ideas, services, products, or books—without metaphors is like driving a Ferrari without gas: You won't get very far."[23]

Go on a walkabout

Sometimes the best way to think about the company's beliefs is to get out of the office and focus on the gnawing questions. When Patagonia hit a wall and had to rethink its priorities, founder Yvon Chouinard, did just that.

"I took a dozen of our top managers to Argentina, to the

windswept mountains of the real Patagonia, for a walkabout," he explains in his book *Let My People Go Surfing*. "In the course of roaming around those wild lands, we asked ourselves why were in business and what kind of business we wanted Patagonia to be. We talked about the values we had in common, and the shared culture that had brought everyone to Patagonia, Inc., and not another company."[24]

By getting out of the office, walking and talking without distractions, your views are likely to become quite clear, quite quickly. (Patagonia decided to stay small and run a business that supported the employees' beliefs in principles such as environmentalism and sustainability.)

Chapter 5

Nine themes that always get people talking

O kay. We've uncovered beliefs and perspectives we believe strongly in (emotion), that are relevant to our audiences, fit into our customers' context, and support our business strategy. The heavy lifting is over.

This chapter explains how to put these views through one more filter for "talk worthiness." You'll also learn how to use the The Nine Block Conversation Planner™ to accomplish the following tasks:

* Translate conventional marketing messages into conversational points of view
* Create program ideas worth talking about
* Brainstorm "talk shorthand" that will help people better understand the company's business perspectives
* Jump-start ideas for speeches, podcasts, or sales presentations
* Think of story ideas to talk about with media or to blog about
* Help shape agendas for planning meetings

There are nine themes that people talk about the most, particularly in business. I arrived at them by tracking and categorizing business communications and business media feature stories over the past ten years. I looked at the types of stories that the media covers the most, aside from hard news and product introductions, the themes of speeches at conferences that generate the most discussion during breaks, the blog postings that catch and get linked from blog to blog, and meeting agendas that perk people up and get them involved.

The emerging patterns from this nonscientific research fall into nine areas:

The Nine Block Conversation Planner™

Aspirations and beliefs	David vs. Goliath	Avalanche about to roll
Anxieties	Counterintuitive/ Contrarian	Personalities
How-to	Glitz and Glam	Seasonal/Event-Related

Aspirations and beliefs

More than any other topic, people want to talk about aspirations and beliefs—and bounce ideas around about how those big ideas might be realized. (This may be why religion is the most popular word-of-mouth topic, ever.)

We want something to believe in that helps us see a company or an issue in a new way. In fact, my research has found that aspirations and beliefs are, hands down, the most "talkable" conversation topics.

"You need to really understand your beliefs and what they're saying to you so that you can be an evangelist for your business," explains architect Chuck Dietsche. "In my field we all—from the architect and client to the roofer and carpenter—want to believe we're creating something more than just a house. To me there's the architecture of aspiration and architecture of accommodation. I market aspirations, the home as a personal spiritual haven, whether it reminds you of grandma's house or the camp on the lake from your childhood."[1]

Sun Microsystems' focus on sharing and ending the digital divide is also an example of a belief-based point of view.

Yvon Chouinard, founder and owner of Patagonia, has led his company and reshaped the outdoor clothing market by talking about aspirations.

In the 1980s, Chouinard talked about his beliefs in how companies could grow by reducing pollution and creating more sustainable business strategies. This led to many innovations, such as developing recycled polyester for use in Patagonia's Synchilla fleece. His environmental views also helped attract a loyal customer base that is equally as passionate about environmentalism.

It's important to note here that Chouinard didn't adopt his environmental platform as a marketing strategy. He did it because he believed in it. All effective and sustainable points of view, like environmental initiatives, must be authentic and believed in. Otherwise they're just more empty campaign slogans.

Chouinard's belief is that companies, like people, can be extraordinary if they are true to themselves and don't exceed their limits.

"You push the envelope and you live for those moments when you're right on the edge, but you don't go over," he explained in his book *Let My People Go Surfing*. "You have to be true to yourself; you have to know your strengths and limitations and live within your means. The same is true for a business. The sooner a company tries to be what it is not, the sooner it tries to 'have it all,' the sooner it will die."[2]

> ✎ *Aspirations are helpful because they engender feelings and help people engage with a company on more of an emotional level. They help us see into a company's soul and understand its bigger cause.*

David vs. Goliath

In the story of David and Goliath, the young Hebrew David took on the Philistine giant Goliath and beat him. It is the way Southwest Airlines conquered the big carriers, the way the once unknown Japanese car manufacturers took on Detroit, the way individuals' podcasts are taking on the media giants, or the way Microsoft took on IBM in the 1980s and has become the Goliath to countless small software Davids.

Sharing stories about how a small organization is taking on a big company is great business sport. A recent Google search of "Business David vs. Goliath," brings up more than half a billion items, from articles in *Forbes* and *Business Week* to every kind of trade publication to popular blog postings. The David versus Goliath story is popular in every industry, nearly everywhere in the world.

Rooting for the underdog grabs our emotions, creates meaning, and invokes passion; we like to listen to the little guy talk about how he's going to win and why the world—or the industry—will be a better place for it.

Here are some examples:

• *Amazon taking on traditional megabookstores.* "If you've read the stories about Amazon.com's growing-up years, you'd be like me—inspired. Bezos is an inspiration to entrepreneurs and small businesses. His story shows that even a David can beat a Goliath in these modern times." Isabelle Chan, senior editor, CNET/Asia.[3]

• *Small hotels slaying the big hotel giants.* "This summer I had the good fortune of sitting with some of the best and brightest minds in hospitality technology, from the smaller hotel chains [to] some of the biggest brands in the industry. What I learned was that the 'little guy' or small hotel operator/management company is better armed today with online customer relationship management arsenals and strategies than are the 'big boys,'" explains Don Hay, CEO of Ft. Worth, Texas-based Digital Alchemy, a customer-relationship management and electronic-marketing company.[4]

• *Network Appliance taking on storage industry giant EMC.* Network Appliance has used a David versus Goliath platform to talk about ways it is challenging computer storage industry giant EMC. Whether talking to analysts, customers, sales reps, or the media, CEO Daniel Warmenhoven is consistent in his tough underdog war cry, "In the end we will push EMC into a corner."[5]

• *Hyundai vs. Mercedes and BMW.* This might seem like a stretch, but Korea's largest carmaker is revving up to take on the luxury car market. "Amid the riches-to-rags tales in the auto industry, Hyundai Motor Co. stands out for moving in the other direction," wrote Moon Ihlwan in *Business Week*. "Now Hyundai is hitting the accelerator again. In 2007 Hyundai will roll out a true luxury model, boasting a powerful 4.6 liter engine to make it a rival to the BMW 5 series."[6]

• *The Red Sox vs. the Yankees.* Oh, that's right. The Sox finally did win the World Series. The point here is that for one hundred years, the Red Sox has been the team for diehard fans who love the game of baseball, who believe that the underdog always has a chance, who see their team as a David to the New York Yankees Goliath.

> ✎ **The David versus Goliath story is a classic, evergreen theme that taps into our deep-seated love for the underdog.**

Avalanche about to roll

We're a world of wannabe insiders. We want to talk about the next big thing coming. We want to hear it first and be able to be the person who tells others. We want to be a smart organization, get the inside scoop on emerging trends, and factor it into our business plans ahead of our competitors. Or get out of a business area about to be massively changed, and not for the better. Sort of like playing the stock market—you want good information early to see opportunities and to prevent risk.

I call this theme "avalanche about to roll." The mountain is rumbling, the sun is getting stronger, but the rocks and snow are yet to fall. You want to tune in to the topic because you know that there's at least a one-in-five chance that you will be killed if caught unaware.

Charles Schwab started his company by listening to rumbling market conversations about investing. The avalanche about to roll was that the middle class was growing more interested in buying stocks, especially as companies were cutting out pensions and more people were beginning to control their own retirement savings through IRAs and 401ks.

In seminars, during media interviews, and on television advertisements, Charles Schwab talked about owning stock, about why anyone could get rich in the stock market, about coming regulatory changes that would make it more possible for the "everyman" to own stocks.

When the SEC deregulated fixed brokerage commissions on May 1, 1975, traditional brokerage firms like Merrill Lynch raised trading fees for individual investors while Schwab lowered its commissions by more than 50 percent. Appealing to the middle-class avalanche, now beginning to move en masse, Schwab was also one of the first brokerage companies to force the mutual funds—and not the clients—to pick up trading fees and the first discounter to create a branch network.

The avalanche rolled, a new investor class was born, and Charles Schwab became one of the most successful discount brokerage firms in the industry—by appealing to the middle class with pragmatic financial advice and using a nonjargon straight talk style.

Microsoft almost got buried by the Internet avalanche or the "Internet Tidal Wave," as CEO Bill Gates called it in his two-page 1995 memo assessing the Internet challenge to Microsoft.

More recently, Ray Ozzie, a Microsoft chief technical officer, whipped up internal and external Microsoft conversations around another avalanche about to roll. In a seven-page, five-thousand-word memo titled "The Internet Services Disruption," Ozzie assessed the trend in Internet services, analyzed the competition, and provided ideas on how Microsoft needs to change to respond to the avalanche. "It's clear that if we fail to do so, our business as we know it is at risk," Ozzie wrote. "We must respond quickly and decisively."

The e-mail was at first sent to fewer than one hundred Microsoft senior managers and engineers, but it was quickly resent throughout the company, to the media, and posted on the Web.

Microsoft has used memos like Ozzie's and Gates's to stir up the market conversation and to educate and rally its people to combat major competitive challenges. They know early warnings of pending massive change. Call it an avalanche or tidal wave, their themes generate interest, debate, fear, excitement, and lots of talk.

> ✎ *Big, emerging trends that could damage a business or industry practice wake people up and fuel discussions about what's coming and what it might mean.*

Anxieties

Fear, apprehension, uncertainty, doubt—we should know about this or something bad might happen.

Anxiety is a cousin of the avalanche about to roll, but it is more about uncertainty than an emerging, disruptive trend.

"We are in all matters more swiftly motivated by fear than appreciation of the good," explained *New York Times* writer Max Frankel. "This is the way we are made," wrote Hans Jonas, the German philosopher, as quoted by Richard Wolin in *The New Republic*. "An evil forces its perception on us by its mere presence, whereas the beneficial can be present unobtrusively and remain unperceived, unless we reflect on it."[7]

In other words, if we don't feel threatened and scared, we tend not to pay attention.

This is a reason why some media use sensationalist, fear-inducing stories to build their audiences. Or why some politicians and religious zealots prey on people's deep-seated fears. They frame their views in the doom and gloom that may come to pass unless people support their views.

The classic anecdote, "You'll never get fired for buying IBM," was based on anxieties. If I buy a little-known technology and it bombs, I'll be fired for it. If I hire IBM and the technology fails, IBM will be blamed, not me.

You can also use anxiety more proactively, for positive change purposes, not just scare tactics. Many inventors and scientists, for example, are anxious that the academic and financial support for scientific innovation is lagging in the United States, trailing behind China, South Korea, and Taiwan.

"The scientific and technical building blocks of our economic leadership are eroding at a time when many other nations are gathering strength," the National Academy of Sciences observed in a recent report. "We fear the abruptness with which a lead in science and technology can be lost—and the difficulty of recovering a lead once lost, if indeed it can be regained at all. . . . For the first time in generations, the nation's children could face poorer prospects than their parents and grandparents did."[8]

"The inventiveness of individuals depends on the context, including sociopolitical, economic, cultural, and institutional factors," said Merton C. Flemings, a professor emeritus at MIT who holds twenty-eight patents and oversees the Lemelson-MIT Program for inventors. "We remain one of the most inventive countries in the world. But all the signs suggest that we won't retain that pre-eminence much longer. The future is very bleak, I'm afraid."[9]

Other examples of anxiety themes abound. Financial services companies urging baby boomers to hurry up and invest more for retirement: "You're 55. Will you have your needed $3.2 million to retire comfortably?" Health care providers urging us to exercise and eat better or suffer a compromised lifestyle, or worse. Tutoring companies planting seeds of doubt about whether our children will score well enough on the SATs to get into a good college. Home security firms warning of increased neighborhood thefts because it's so easy to break into most homes.

Although anxiety themes are effective, some people are becoming more skeptical of these approaches, so it's important to back up anxiety themes with facts to prove the point.

> ✎ *Fear and anxiety themes grab people's attention. But the overuse of the practice has exacerbated consumer skepticism. Use it wisely by backing up your views with facts to justify the threat and explain the possible ramifications.*

Contrarian/counterintuitive/ challenging assumptions

These three themes are like first cousins, similar in many ways but slightly different.

Contrarian perspectives defy conventional wisdom; they are positions that often are not in line with—or may even be directly opposite to—the wisdom of the crowd. For example, when most investors dump their stocks, contrarian investors buy, buy, buy!

Counterintuitive ideas fight with what our intuition (as opposed to a majority of the public) says is true. When you introduce counterintuitive ideas, it takes people a minute to reconcile the objective truth with their gut assumption about the topic. For instance, when the company Endeca says it's a "find company" not a "search company," what does that mean? Isn't searching about finding?

Challenging widely held assumptions means, for example, when everyone else says the reason for an event is X, you show that it's actually Y. For instance, a recent study proved that workplace stress does *not* lead to high blood pressure. There are many people who experience workplace stress *and* high blood pressure, but their high blood pressure is caused by other factors—heredity, poor eating habits, alcohol consumption, obesity, and so forth—not the stress they experience at work. The challenge jolts our thinking and gets us to listen closely and get involved in the dialogue.

Sometimes, shaking things up offends people so much that any good intentions are obliterated. That's what happened to former Harvard University President Larry Summers when he spoke about diversifying the science and engineering workforce at a National Bureau of Economic Research conference.[10] Summers offered his hypothesis for the gender gap—and promptly set off international outrage about his views.

Summers offered three possible reasons why there are more men than women in science and engineering careers, and backed up each reason with data, as all good scientists do. The biggest reason, he suggested, was that fewer women than men are willing to spend eighty hours a week away from their children. The second reason, which became the most controversial after the speech, was that more boys than girls tend to score very high or very low on high school math tests, producing a similar average but a higher proportion of scores in the top percentiles, which leads to high-powered academic careers in science and engineering. The third reason was discrimination by universities. Summers said repeatedly that Harvard and other schools should work to eliminate discrimination.

Sounds rational. So why did so many people react so vehemently to the speech? I would suggest style more than content.

Summers likes to provoke people to get them into the type of intellectual food fights that generate meaty discussions. He is a classic contrarian—arrogant, intense, challenging, and insightful.

At the beginning and end of his controversial speech, Summers even acknowledged that he wanted to provoke the audience. "I asked Richard, when he invited me to come here and speak, whether he wanted an institutional talk about Harvard's policies toward diversity or whether he wanted some questions asked and some attempts at provocation, because I was willing to do the second and didn't feel like doing the first," he stated.

He added, "Let me just conclude by saying that I've given you my best guesses after a fair amount of reading the literature and a lot of talking to people. They may be all wrong. I will have served my purpose if I have provoked thought on this question and provoked the marshalling of evidence to contradict what I have said. But I think we all need to be thinking very hard about how to do better on these issues and that they are too important to sentimentalize rather than to think about in as rigorous and careful ways as we can."[11]

Provoke, provoke, provoke. This approach works effectively in some contexts, but perhaps not in the context of Ivy League universities.

Another contrarian view that has provoked discussion, although not as widespread as Summers, is the book series *Can Asians Think?* by former Singapore diplomat Kishore Mahbubani.[12] Although Mahbubani offers no answers, his questions provoke conversations about widely held assumptions about Asians.

"The conventional wisdom that Asians cherish learning is misleading," wrote *Time Asia* magazine writer Sin-Ming Shaw in reviewing the book. "In the past, learning meant passing imperial exams that led to well-paid jobs in the civil service. It's not altogether different in modern Asia. Learning for its own sake is considered a luxury if not a financial waste, unless it also leads to an attractive income stream."[13]

Brad Anderson, CEO of Best Buy, takes a more counterintuitive than contrarian approach. When Best Buy announced it was going to fire some of its customers, people stopped and said, "What? Customers fire businesses; businesses don't fire their own customers." But Best Buy has a counterintuitive perspective.

In explaining why the company was firing some customers, Anderson said he wanted to separate the "angel" customers from the "devil" customers. He described the "devils" as the company's worst customers; they only buy the loss leaders, they make the company match lower advertised prices so they know they're getting the absolute lowest price; and some even buy products, apply for rebates, and then return the products for a refund. "I'm probably a bit of a rebel," he said. "So I admire leaders with a point of view that is not conventionally held."[14]

McDonald's CEO Jim Skinner thinks that challenging assumptions and reframing conversations is a strategic necessity. "We've challenged assumptions that others make about us. It's not as a defensive play—we know that's a losing proposition. But because when you accept assumptions, you limit your ability to develop sustainable solutions to the issues," Skinner explained at the 2005 Business for Social Responsibility Conference. "By changing the framework of the debate, we've driven better business practices, enhanced trust, improved business results, and helped us be a better company, more socially responsible company."[15]

McDonald's has challenged the following three stereotypes:

1. McDonald's marketing to children is harmful to kids.
2. The quality of McDonald's food and nutrition is questionable.
3. The fast-food giant offers low-paying, dead-end jobs.

"I tell our people, 'Do not get arrogant,' 'Do not be prescriptive,'" said Skinner. "Our role is to weigh in on the debate and educate. As leaders, we are subject to greater scrutiny in everything that we do," added Skinner. "But we should not let this hold us back from taking on the issues of making changes that have some controversy, even if we have to challenge stereotypes and myths. If it doesn't have controversy, it probably won't be worth changing."[16]

✎ *The boldness of contrarian views grabs attention; the more original and less arrogant they are, the more useful they will be in provoking meaningful conversations. Framing views counter to how we intuitively think about topics—going against natural "gut instincts"— pauses and then resets how we think and talk about concepts. Challenging assumptions is good for debate and discussion, and especially important in protecting corporate reputation.*

Personalities and personal stories

There's nothing more interesting than a personal story with some life lessons to help us understand what makes executives tick and what they value the most. The points of these personal stories are remembered, retold, and instilled into company lore. Plus, our society loves stories about "personalities," including business leaders.

Robert Goizueta, the respected CEO of Coca-Cola who died of lung cancer in 1997, said he hated giving speeches, but he was always telling stories, often personal ones about how he and his family left Cuba when Castro took control. "The only property I was allowed to bring with me into this country was my education. It is a powerful and uniquely American idea that a young immigrant could come to this country with nothing but a good education and thirty years later have the opportunity to lead one of the world's best-known enterprises."[17]

Burger King's former CEO Greg Brenneman credits growing up as a Mennonite farm boy in Kansas, getting up to bale hay at 6 A.M., as what instilled the values and work ethic that helped him first to turn around Continental Airlines, and then tackle Burger King's challenges. "I got more out of the farm than Harvard Business School," he has said.[18]

When Steve Jobs gave the commencement address to Stanford University in June 2005, he shared his personal story and life lessons. That commencement address was e-mailed around the world, posted on Web sites, discussed on blogs, talked about at business meetings, and featured verbatim in *Fortune* magazine.

He talked about love and loss, death, connecting the dots, what he has always wished for himself, and what he wished for the graduating class.

"When I was young, there was an amazing publication called *The Whole Earth Catalog*, which was one of the bibles of my generation. Stewart [Stewart Brand, editor of *Whole Earth*] and his team put out several issues of *The Whole Earth Catalog*, and then, when it had run its course, they put out a final issue," said Jobs.

"It was the mid-1970s and I was your age. On the back cover of their final issue was a photograph of an early-morning country road, the kind you might find yourself hitchhiking on if you were so adventurous. Beneath it were the words: 'Stay Hungry. Stay Foolish.' It was their farewell message as they signed off. Stay Hungry. Stay Foolish. And I have always wished that for myself. And now, as you graduate to begin anew, I wish that for you. Stay Hungry. Stay Foolish."[19]

> ✎ *People want to talk about people. Good personal stories that help people feel good about an executive and his or her organization are good for business.*

How-to

How-to stories and advice are classics. Theoretical and thought-provoking ideas are nice, but people love pragmatic how-to anecdotes about how to solve problems, get ahead, make friends, and influence people.

To be conversation-worthy, how-to themes need to be fresh and original, providing a new twist to what people already know. For example, in talking with female customers and doing research, Home Depot was surprised to find that women initiate a big percentage of home improvement projects. So the company started how-to clinics and do-it-herself workshops that have been attended by more than 200,000 women.[20]

Here are some how-to examples that companies have talked about:

* From a business analytics software company: "A change from a hands-off approach to hands-on management."
* From a management consulting company during the dot-com mania: "How to use rational approaches for managing in an irrational e-world."
* From an innovation consulting firm: "How to escape 'The Big Idea' hell and get more ideas off the whiteboard and into the real world."

* From a mobile media company: "Five ways to win with mobile commerce."
* From Genuity CEO's Paul Gudonis: Dot-Bomb Lessons—ten lessons learned in the Internet boom and bust.

> ✎ *How-to views, including advice and lessons,*
> *provide people with pragmatic ideas that they*
> *can put to work to solve immediate problems.*
> *To stand out, make sure your ideas are fresh,*
> *insightful, and maybe even sprinkled with a bit*
> *of counterintuitive wisdom.*

Glitz and glam

Robert Palmer sang about being addicted to love. Our society is even more addicted to glamour and celebrity. Finding a way to link a point of view to something glitzy and glamorous is a sure-fire conversation starter.

Although I don't have much interest in hedge funds, I did pay attention to the topic when *Forbes* published an article asking, "What do Barbra Streisand, Senator Robert Torricelli, and Bianca Jagger have in common? They have all lost money investing in hedge funds."[21]

Sun Microsystems created a text-messaging program that allows audiences at U2's rock concerts to get a text message from Bono on their mobile phones after the concert, sending them to the One Campaign Web site. (The One Campaign is a movement to end AIDS and poverty in Africa.) Certainly something for Sun and its customers to talk about, especially because the program used the company's technology and supported its corporate point of view.

Tagging on to the widespread interest in the Academy Awards, Randall Rothenberg, director of intellectual property at consultancy Booz Allen-Hamilton, crafted a point of view about the similarity between creating new "star" brands and movie stars. Pointing to the Academy Award nominees for best actor—Philip Seymour Hoffman, Terrence Howard, Heath Ledger, Joaquin Phoenix, and David Straithairn—Rothenberg said, "However prodigious their talents, few would argue that a Cary Grant—or even a mid-career Harrison Ford—will ever emerge from this bunch. There is not a Colgate in this bunch. We are entering an era in which the best we can hope for is a Tom's of Maine."[22]

Even if our businesses and stories aren't directly connected to the glitz and the glam, there's often a way to get a rub-off effect.

When the *New York Times* came out with a business story about how Sarah Jessica Parker was working with her financial adviser to invest her money,[23] I wondered why my financial adviser, a woman, wouldn't send that article to her female clients with a note saying something like, "I know you want to build the same kind of security as Parker (even if you don't have a *Sex & the City* salary). Here are a couple of points in the article that, I, too, use in managing your money."

Another approach is to find lessons from celebrity CEOs who are relevant to your industry. For example, if you were selling collaboration software and consulting services, you could interview well-known people whose success depends on collaboration, like a movie director, music producer, or athletic coach.

You might also choose to frame your value in a glamorous way. For example, as was discussed earlier in this book, American

Canadian Caribbean cruise line talks about how traveling on its ships is like cruising on a friend's yacht. Wouldn't it be interesting for the company to share stories about the adventures of the rich and famous cruising on one another's yachts?

> ✎ *We're instantly drawn to stories about celebrities and parallels between our more mundane business world and that of the glamorous entertainment industry. The glitz and the glam are fun and fabulous. They give us a lot to talk about with many people.*

Seasonal/event-related

Tying into seasonal or major events has a limited shelf life. But these themes, done right, may appeal to sales reps looking for something interesting to talk to customers about. Seasonal and event-related topics can be used in weekly voice mails to employees, or featured in departmental or company-wide presentations. Public relations people can use these themes when talking with the media, such as the following examples:

* Industry predictions around the New Year.
* Tax and financial advice in March and April.
* Motivational advice or insights on "coaching" employees for extraordinary performance around the time of the Super Bowl, the World Series, or another major sporting event. Draw analogies between managing professional athletes and high-performance employees.

* Advice on how to use new technologies to stay connected on summer vacations. (Or advice from mental-health experts on how *not* to stay connected on summer vacations.)
* All things related to kids in late August and September while we're getting them back to school and planning for the new school year.
* For project managers at election time: a behind-the-scenes look at the ultimate project—managing a fast-paced, complex political campaign.

> ✎ *Talking about ideas tied to events is a well-used, proven strategy. That's why it showed up in the research about common themes that people talk about. To me, it's the least interesting of the nine block themes because these events come and go so quickly, and the event-related technique is such a common marketing practice. However, it's a proven short-term strategy.*

The Nine Block framework speeds thinking and planning. Of all the techniques in this book, Nine Block, more than any other, helps marketers find something to talk about. Use it to come up with points of view, ideas for sound bites, speech topics, articles to write, or content to develop for your Web site.

The chart in Figure 5-1 illustrates how some of the points of view discussed in this book map to the Nine Block Conversation Planner™.

The Nine Block Conversation Planner™
Examples

Aspirations & Beliefs	David vs. Goliath	Avalanche about to roll
Sharing technology will end the digital divide. Women deserve to be treated with absolute dignity.	The small hotel operator is better armed than the "big boys." Hyundai takes on Mercedes, BMW in luxury car market.	The Internet tidal wave The Internet services disruption
Anxieties	**Counterintuitive/Contrarian**	**Personalities**
The United States' scientific and technical building blocks are eroding while other nations are gathering strength.	We're not a search company, we're a find company. We're firing some customers, separating the angel customers from the devil customers.	Stay hungry. Stay foolish. The only property I was allowed to bring with me into this country was my education.
How to	**Glitz and Glam**	**Seasonal/Event-Related**
Ten lessons learned in the Internet boom and bust A hands-off approach to hands-on management	Traveling on our ships is just like cruising on a friend's yacht. Investing like Sarah Jessica Parker The lack of "star" brands: movie stars and product stars	Marketing lessons from the Red Sox How to stay connected on summer vacation Business predictions for the New Year

Figure 5-1.

Chapter 6

Straight talk: Talk like you talk, talk like you mean it, talk in these ten new ways

Why is it often so difficult to figure out how to bring our ideas to life?

The short answer is that we often haven't thought through our idea. We're not clear in our own heads about the purpose of what we want to communicate. The longer answer is that sometimes—consciously and unconsciously—we fall into the following traps:

* We haven't taken the time to talk with customers or executives to understand what they want to hear or how they think about the topic.
* We start writing or talking about something we don't really understand or believe in. We put down the words, but lacking context and belief, the words are meaningless.
* We try to force ourselves to adopt some style that is supposed to be businesslike or the "brand voice," but it's not *our* style, so we get blocked and frustrated and end up talking or

writing in ways that include all the business buzz words but lack a human voice.

* We fall back on well-worn organizational ideas and language, not wanting to stir things up too much.

Are we speaking Doglish?

Our communications often comes across as if we're speaking a kind of marketing "Doglish."[1] We're working hard to convince people just how transformational, revolutionary, innovative, and industry-leading our products are. But customers often ignore us—or, more precisely, they ignore our marketing messages—because we're just not speaking their language.

It's like the relationship between humans and dogs that Patricia McConnell, adjunct assistant professor of zoology at the University of Wisconsin-Madison, writes about in her book *The Other End of the Leash.* "Although humans and dogs share a re-markable relationship that is unique in the animal world, we are still two entirely different species." she says. "Quite simply, humans are primates and dogs are canids. Since we each speak a different native tongue, a lot gets lost in the translation."[2]

A lot gets lost in business communications, as well, even though we and our customers are the same species.

Back in the 1990s, when Jacques Nasser was CEO of Ford Motor Company, he went into the field, meeting with small groups of senior executives to talk about shareholder value and what that means in daily business. After several meetings he experienced the Doglish problem. Despite his genuine passion and commitment to fostering greater understanding of his strategy, his executives didn't know what he was talking about.

"I spent hours talking about financial ratios," he said. "But it wasn't until someone was brave enough to come up to me afterward and say, 'What's a P/E ratio?' that I realized why so few people in the company were thinking about shareholder value. They didn't understand it as a concept."[3]

Eventually, Ford began business literacy training to reduce the translation problems between Nasser and his managers.

Sometimes misunderstanding is a business literacy or language problem. Sometimes it's because people aren't interested in what we think they should be interested in. Other times, we're just not very excited about our own topic.

As Autodesk CEO Carol Bartz has said, "If you're not excited, how can you get others excited? People will know. It's like how kids and dogs can sense when people don't like them."[4]

Screenwriter Robert McKee, who advises corporations like Microsoft as well as filmmakers, believes that telling too rosy a story actually works against businesses. "You can send out a press release talking about increased sales and a bright future, but your audience knows it's never that easy. . . . Positive hypothetical pictures and boilerplate press releases actually work against you because they foment distrust among the people you're trying to convince."[5]

Reset business communications style

This morning a marketing director called to share this bit of information: "The CEO really likes how you've positioned us. It's clear, accurate, and easy to talk about," he said. "How did you do it?"

The secret is to ask good questions and listen carefully to the CEO's tone and style. Often we think there's a need to use corporate language instead of using the language that people speak.

Does any person ever really say those quotes that we see in so many press releases? Let's not make writing so difficult. Let's use people's beliefs, words, style, and sentiments. Plain, honest, human language—real words that real people use in everyday conversations. One reason blogging took off so quickly is that blogs are written the way real people speak, and people like listening to real people.

Instead of writing to be read, write to be said. Or edit down what someone said, letting people "hear" the person's voice and style. Communications today doesn't need to be perfectly written or produced in slick formats. We need to spend less time on producing perfect marketing "stuff," and more time communicating in the plain-speak of conversations. The goal is not to be perfect, but to be understood.

Sounds easy, but it's difficult to change. In school and during our careers, we have been taught to write to be read. We were punished for incomplete sentences, slang, and fragments. And, please, omit all passion. That's not how it's done.

In fact, it wasn't so many years ago that I got a negative performance review for being too passionate in client meetings and in my communications approach. Clients liked the work and they liked me, but my boss thought that I should adopt a more "executive, businesslike" communications style. That's what would be required, the alpha fraidy cat said, for me to be promoted. So I quit and my clients came with me, following the passion.

But I digress.

The point is that we live in a talk world and we don't usually talk in grammatically correct sentences. Communications today is about the ear. Writing for the ear and using the ear more to listen to what people are telling us.

So it's not only all right but in many ways it is better to change our style.

Ten ways to get on the straight-talk wagon

Here are ten small ways to break bad habits and move into a new conversational talk style. I'm sure you know these tips, so treat this section as a quick review.

1. What's the point?

What are we trying to help people understand? Why should they care? Why is it relevant? What's new or different that you have to say about it? How will the ideas affect the listener?

In the world of marketing, communications often seems muddled. Competing company Web sites say the same things. Presenters at conferences blur. Sales presentations numb. Webinars drag. All because they're throwing a lot of information at us, but lack a point.

One way to clarify your point is to start a conversation, e-mail, meeting, or speech by saying, "My intent is to help you understand why _____." Or, "My intent is for us to try to figure out why _____ ." Or, "Here's why I, personally, think this point matters: _____." Articulating the intent helps clarify the point.

Always start with a point.

2. Don't be afraid to use the first person

The easiest way to adopt a conversational style is to include the first person "I" in your communications. Although it may give some English and journalism teachers the jitters, I promise that when used appropriately, the first person will liberate your communications.

When I'm in meetings, I use the first person to talk about what I think. When I write blogs, I use the first person to share ideas. What about presentations, phone calls, e-mails? All in the first person.

Bob Wyss, a staff writer at the *Providence Journal*, wrote about how uncomfortable it is to shift from the anonymous third person to the first, and yet, in the end, how it makes the story more interesting. "First-person stories always draw far more comments than third person. It is one of the few times readers notice the writer and the byline."[6]

A Harvard Business School "Working Knowledge" review of the book *More Space: Nine Antidotes to Complacency in Business* criticized the writers' use of the first person, yet acknowledged that the form made the book engaging. "Some of the writing here is self-absorbed—the most used letter in the *More Space* alphabet is 'I,'" wrote Sean Silverthorne. "But the risk-taking with form and content ultimately pays off in a very readable, fresh, and insightful collection." He added, "There is a passion for work and business that comes through."[7]

People want fresh and insightful. Add more of the first person—"we," "us," and "I"—and you'll deliver fresh and insightful marketing communications better than you would with the anonymous, impersonal third person "him," "her," and "them."

3. Create more sound bites and let them go free

Sound bites help people remember and talk about a point of view—more so than speaking points, messaging documents, elevator speeches, or any other form of communications. These short, punchy phrases are a shortcut to understanding.

Take points of view, turn them into sound bites, and let them go free—to the sales organization, public relations department, investor relations staff, customers, analysts, executives. They'll love you for it because sound bites help them tell a story, convey the company's value, and show why the organization is different.

Sound bites provide a Cliffs Notes™-like summary of an idea, a strategy, or a story. Some briefly tell the story. Others proclaim a cause, provoke discussion, question assumptions, summarize your value proposition, or use a metaphor to help explain. They are tools to draw people into discussions or to help you quickly convey your point. Some are witty and metaphorical; others simple but memorable.

* "Saegis is out to find the 'Viagra of the Brain.'" Saegis Pharmaceuticals, which is developing drugs to treat brain-based diseases like Alzheimer's.
* "Clean, safe, reliable. That's how to make money in the airline business." The mantra of Gordon Bethune when he was running Continental Airlines.
* "It's the economy, stupid." Bill Clinton's 1992 campaign mantra, focusing his campaign staff on voters' chief concern—economic insecurity.
* "Bring humanity back to air travel." JetBlue.
* "When tires fail, drivers should be able to pull over, not roll over." James Lampe, president, Bridgestone/Firestone.
* "If you make over $300,000 a year, this tax cut means you get to buy a new Lexus. If you make $50,000 a year, you get to buy a new muffler on your used car." Senator Tom Daschle.
* "To control market conversations, improve the conversations." Hugh MacLeod, blogging expert and consultant.
* "Online customer communities are like customer advisory groups on steroids." Diane Hessan, CEO, Communispace.
* "Real women have curves." Dove.

* "We're going to eliminate the digital divide." Sun Microsystems' CEO Scott McNealy.
* "The medium is the message." Author Marshall McLuhan.
* "If it doesn't fit, you must acquit." Lead OJ Simpson defense attorney Johnnie Cochran.

The test for a sound bite is that people make meaning from it. They have a better understanding of your perspective or unique position after hearing it. Marketers need many sound bites to help people understand multiple aspects of their company. In this way they are not tag lines.

As an aside, tag lines too often are so general and vague that they end up saying nothing about a company; they don't help you understand anything. I've seen three organizations use "Now more than ever" as tag lines. Two completely unrelated businesses use, "Wouldn't it be great?" What does that mean? It doesn't help me understand anything.

Sound bites help in engaging people in conversations. Don't try to force them to be all-purpose tag lines. For that matter, try to foster understanding by spending more time creating sound bites than tag lines. After all, on any given day, more people may talk about your company than read or watch its ads. Yet businesses spend a disproportionate amount of time and budget creating tag lines.

Some sound bites are clever, some are straightforward. Most are ten words or less. Some are just three mantra-like words. All should help people better understand the point of view.

4. Cut to the chase, say less

Get to the point. Keep sentences short. Say less. Edit judiciously. Ask more questions. Use more pictures. Length and heft have little to do with value. Make sense?

5. Get help from your invisible friend

Many three-year-olds make sense of their worlds by talking to invisible, imaginary friends. The same approach can help marketers. Step back and think about how you'd start a conversation with a real person who is likely to buy the product or service.

For example, when I'm working with technology clients, I think of my neighbor Keith, who is a chief information officer of a multibillion-dollar company. Thinking about what he cares about, how he talks, and just how skeptical he is, helps me avoid jargon and focus on the one point he would find most interesting to talk about.

I imagine having a conversation with Keith. "Hey, Keith, what do you think of this new technology?" That's the helpful starting point. Sounds kind of juvenile. But it helps us mentally ditch the old all-about-the-company-nothing-about-the-customer style of corporate-speak.

6. Tell more stories

Stories are the oldest form of spoken communications. Use them more. People like, remember, and enjoy talking about stories in conversations.

"Stories are the large and small instruments of meaning, of explanation, that we store in our memories. We cannot live without them," says Joe Lambert, director of the nonprofit Center of Digital Storytelling. "So why is it that when many of us are asked to construct a story as a formal presentation to illustrate a point, we go blank?"[8]

One reason we go blank is that we try to make our stories say everything—and end up not saying much at all. Marketers often try to jam every product feature and benefit into customer stories. The stories end up more like convoluted, corporate-talk case studies—neither interesting nor memorable.

Stories don't have to be larger than life, showing how the company faced a dramatic turning point, summoned heroic courage, and succeeded where none have triumphed before. Many good stories are small personal stories that illustrate a point.

In fact, sometimes stories work better when they're less abundant, illustrating one company value, one unique product feature, one particularly appealing point of view, or how far your company goes to deliver on its promises.

A story that's became legend at Sapient, a business and IT consulting firm, is how the company went to the mat to help a competitor meet a mutual client's deadline—all because of Sapient's brand promise to deliver the right business results on time and on budget.

Sapient and one of its competitors were working side by side on a large, complex IT project for a major corporation. Each was responsible for doing a part of the project. The project depended on both firms implementing their part of the job. But as the client deadline loomed, Sapient realized that the other consulting firm had incorrectly scoped the project and was going to miss the deadline.

Instead of explaining to the client that the other company had messed up and that was why the project would take longer, Sapient, quietly and on its own dime (or tens of thousands of dimes), assigned several of its people to help the competitor. Both company teams worked together, pulling several all-nighters to get the project done by the promised deadline.

The story helps people in the company understand that "on-time, on-budget" is not just a marketing line. It's a core belief. And all employees have the freedom to do whatever it takes to deliver on that belief.

Or consider this legend at Best Buy. "We had helicopters come to dry the pavement so the Detroit location could open on time. That's folklore now," said Steve Prather, vice president of internal communications for Best Buy.[9]

Timberland, the rugged footwear and outerwear company, has always prided itself on being an independent spirit company, doing things differently from its competitors. In explaining how he interviews potential employees to make sure they fit into the company culture, Timberland CEO Jeff Schwartz tells the story of how he asks job candidates to dress passionately and wear their favorite outfit (but no Timberlands!) to interviews with him. Schwartz says, "Once I had a guy show up in a really tight navy-blue suit. He said, 'I got married in this suit. . . . I remember every single instant of my wedding.' I said, 'I love this guy!' I can't wait to have a creative discussion with him, because he's going to fight for what he believes in."[10]

How to capture and share more stories, more easily? Here are two simple ways.

First, give people a few questions to help them tell stories. Try not to use the typical, boring business questions such as "How did your company benefit from using the Acme router?" Or, "How would you quantify the return on your investment with us?"

Instead, use questions that open people up to sharing more specifics and more feelings. (Remember, emotion is the super-highway to meaning making.)

* "What surprised you the most about changing the way you do X?"
* "What does it mean *to you* personally to be able to run your business this way?"

* "Do you really think the change involved was worth it?"
* "How did it make you feel being able to do Y?"
* "Having done it, what advice would you give to people just starting out?"
* "What three words would you use to describe the experience?"
* "Would you recommend it?"
* "What annoyed you about the process?"

The second thing is to select someone to be in charge of collecting and organizing stories. Assign someone in marketing to create a database of company stories and anecdotes and classify them by topic so they're easy for people to find and use. Ask each sales rep to share at least two stories a year, and the CEO to share six.

Set up a special telephone number where people can call in stories as they hear them, otherwise they may forget them. Edit judiciously. Let the real words live. And, like sound bites, let the stories go free, making it easier and more interesting for people to talk about the company.

Hold a digital storytelling workshop at the annual sales or marketing meeting, with a competition among small teams to create two-minute digital movies that tell your value proposition in new ways. At the last day of the meeting, show the team movies and have an *American Idol*–style contest to vote on the three best movies. Then, make copies of the best movies for everyone in the sales force to use with customers.

You will be amazed at the buried talent in your people and the magic that they can create with a 250-word script, digital images, and a soundtrack. The nonprofit Center for Digital Storytelling has helped more than ten thousand people of all ages and backgrounds, and all types of organizations, make these kinds of movies. Our firm produced one of these ten thousand stories. In three days, we learned how to convey what our firm is all about through just 278 words, 12 images, and a funky guitar soundtrack.

Fewer words. More stories.

7. Be sincere and frank

Mean what you say and say what you mean. When in doubt, leave it out. Heeding these old adages still makes sense.

In his book *Winning*, Jack Welch laments that the pervasive lack of candor is "the biggest dirty little secret in business." He explains, "Too many people—too often—instinctively don't express themselves with frankness. They don't communicate straightforwardly or put forth ideas looking to stimulate real debate. But when you've got candor, everything just operates faster and better."[11]

Former New York governor Mario Cuomo, recognized as one of our country's most superb orators, says that sincerity and tapping both the head and the heart are the secret to delivering moving speeches. "The most important thing in oration is to be sincere," he explained. "You don't have to use extravagant metaphors and Kennedy litanies. You don't have to be William Buckley to find the right language. And if you speak only to their hearts and you slight their minds, then they'll come away offended. And if you speak only to their minds, then you don't come away with a moving speech."[12]

Intellectual food fights, candid debates, and frank perspectives help speed understanding. Don't hide behind overly polite language, "safe" topics, and accepted business jargon. It clouds rather than clarifies.

8. Use good headlines

Using a good headline helps in three ways. It forces us to summarize the point of what we want to say. It focuses our ideas for a presentation, or helps shape a meeting agenda. It also helps as a subject line in e-mails, blogs, and online community postings, those highly conversational media that just happen to be written.

A headline isn't meant to be written exactly how we talk. Headlines are shorthand; they lack words we'd use in conversation, but they help readers get the point quickly. The elements of a good headline include the following:

* Grabs attention while also summarizing your point: *Do men lack ambition?* versus *10-year behavioral research study explores male attitudes toward work.*
* Uses present tense, active verb: *Acme Industries nets software contract* (present tense) versus *Software contract netted by Acme Industries* (past tense).
* Is brief: *U2 rocks.*
* Readers get it on the first take: *Read my lips. No new taxes.*
* Provides specifics: *Acme revenues up 18 percent; profits soar to 30 percent* versus *Earnings released at Acme Corporation today.*
* Uses short, common words. *Fed raises rates.*

9. Eliminate worthless buzzwords, phrases, and adjectives

Eliminate the groaners—those overused buzzwords and phrases that add little value. Here are some favorite offenders, collected by writer and public relations adviser Nathan Silverman and featured by BuzzKiller.net, a site formed by business journalists in the late 1990s to showcase the inanity of corporate jargon.

Buzzword, overused adjective	What it really means
Strategic	We do the same stuff as everybody else, but "strategic" sounds impressive.
Aggressive	Given a chance, we'll annoy everybody.
Full-service	We'll try to sell you anything.
Leading supplier	No one has ever heard of us, but if you look at this tiny niche in which we've positioned ourselves, we're practically a Microsoft.
Have-to-have	You folks fell for "peer-to-peer" and "business-to-business," so surely you'll fall for this mumbo jumbo.
Ramping	We're getting ready to introduce a new product, but we're six months behind.
Major breakthrough	We finally figured out how to deliver on all the promises we've been making for the past couple of years.
Robust	This product works big time. It's no weakling, wannabe. Really.

Other business drivel to avoid:

Core competencies
Best practices
24/7
On the ground
Win-win
Results-driven
Empower

Mission-critical
Turnkey
Fast track
Value-added
Synergy
Solutions
All verbs and nonsensical words that have "-ize" tacked
onto them, e.g., "incentivize" and even "utilize" ("use"
works better)

10. Write it down

A late-night talk-show host asked prolific "redneck" comedian
Jeff Foxworthy how he got his material. Foxworthy said that he
watches everyday life and writes everything down.

One of his jokes is: "If you've ever slow danced in a Waffle
House, you might be a redneck." He got the joke one night while
waiting for a table at a Waffle House. "You ever eaten in a Waffle House, like one in the morning?" he asked radio DJ Paul Harris. "You have the people waiting for a booth to open—and if
you're waiting in line at a Waffle House you've had a toddy or
two. The jukebox was playing and I guess this couple got bored
and they started slow dancing and I said, 'Hand me a napkin, I'm
writing that down.' "[13]

Foxworthy believes that more people could write funny material if they just got in the habit of writing things down. Foxworthy jots copious notes and ideas as he sees them. Other
writers use the same technique. That's why they have so much
good material, drawn from real-world observations and events.

The same technique helps in business. Jot down phrases, language, metaphors, stories, and ideas that you hear in conversations as soon as you hear them. Carry index cards and put one
idea on a card as the ideas come. Or set up an idea place in your

PDA. Capture them before they escape. These notes are the clues to what people are talking about—and how they're talking about them, in context and in style.

The language of conversation is the language of understanding

Why include a chapter that reviews much of what we already know about the value of straight talk? Because plain-speak is the language of conversations; conversations are the language of understanding; and creating understanding is the purpose of marketing.

Chapter 7 explores how to deprogram from the "talk at" marketing mentality and adopt a conversational marketing mind-set.

Chapter 7

Shift to a conversational marketing mind-set

If conversational marketing is one of the most effective ways for customers to get to know our companies and to understand our value, what's stopping us from adopting this marketing approach? Two things: One is our mind-set about the purpose of marketing. The other is that some people in our organizations may not believe that conversational marketing makes good business sense. This chapter discusses:

* Five business reasons to change: customers, word-of-mouth marketing, product sameness, reputation, and the integrated marketing stalemate
* Seven ways to deprogram from a command-and-control mind-set: undergo the company/competitor immersion treatment, delete the adjectives, ask new questions, think rapport-like versus report-like, view marketing as the voice of the customer, think of marketing as teaching, and empower customers like employees
* The benefit of losing control

Five business reasons to change to conversational marketing

Admitting that we can't control the message or the channels in which people talk about our companies and products is unsettling. It poses the question: What exactly is marketing's role?

Rather than message developer and distributor, marketing can play a more valuable role in bringing customers' points of view back into the company to help influence products and services that *they* want to buy.

Why change now? The most important reason is that customers want a different type of relationship with companies. They're less interested in companies that promote to them, and more interested in companies that take an interest in them and what *they* want to know and understand. And then, of course, you need to develop product and service experiences that customers want. In a Yankelovich study, 54 percent of customers say they avoid being exposed to marketing, and 56 percent avoid buying products that overwhelm them with marketing.[1] Furthermore, customers don't want relationships to be "managed." Customers stay loyal when they feel emotionally connected to a company. (And, of course, when their experience with the product or service is excellent.) The best way to connect is to talk with customers about what's on *their* minds—and provide perspective and other relevant insights. It makes perfect sense: being "other-oriented" helps build relationships.

Customers rule. That's the big reason to change.

There are four other good business reasons to change marketing practices as well.

1. *Word-of-mouth marketing.* Customers have been providing one another with information and advice for ages. Through

blogs, e-mail, and online communities, people now share recommendations—good and bad—not just with ten or twenty
people, but with thousands. And as the trust research mentioned
in Chapter 1 shows, people trust other people more than they
trust companies.

As a result of this communications tsunami, companies have
begun paying close attention to how they can use word-of-
mouth to achieve their marketing objectives.

Much of the word-of-mouth marketing talk has been about
products. Some experts, like Ed Keller, who wrote *The Influen-
tials,* say that you need a cool product to create buzz. The Word
of Mouth Marketing Association (WOMMA) defines word-of-
mouth marketing as "giving people a reason to talk about your
products and services, and making it easier for that conversation
to take place."[2]

Although a good product—think iPod, or an innovative
business strategy such as eBay—will always get people talking,
we can still gain value from word-of-mouth marketing even if
our company isn't particularly cool or innovative. People want
to—and do—talk about more than just products. They like talking about possibilities. They like sharing war stories and lessons
learned. So, even if our products aren't cool, we can still harness
the power of word-of-mouth marketing by talking about our
beliefs, by sharing our point of view.

If an important goal of marketing is to deepen relationships
and trust, talking with customers about ideas that matter to
them is the way to do just that. Customer-to-company conversations are word-of-mouth marketing on steroids.

2. *Product "sameness."* Marketing and sales execs constantly
grapple with how to differentiate products that are vastly similar to one another. Although search engine optimization, mobile
marketing, and other new channels may amplify a product's

message, they won't set it apart. If you really want to differenti-ate, have something to talk about that is relevant and valuable, something that connects with people on both an emotional and a rational level.

Comments such as, "They're the smartest and best people to do business with," or "I really trust that company," are reasons people choose one vendor over another. You can foster those perceptions—inexpensively and effectively—through conversa-tional marketing. Conversations help customers get to know you—and you them.

3. *Corporate and brand reputation.* Although having a good name is important to companies large and small, many ex-ecutives are uncertain of what communications techniques will improve their companies' reputation.

One way is to talk about what the company believes in, par-ticularly those beliefs or perspectives that are especially rele-vant to your customers—and perhaps unconventional or rarely talked about.

4. *The integrated marketing stalemate.* The debate about just how to make sure that the advertising, public relations, brand-ing, interactive marketing, and sales silos are in synch continues as the concept of integrated marketing wanes. The advertising left hand doesn't know what the public relations right hand is doing, say some. Sales thinks marketing doesn't understand the real busi-ness issues and doesn't give it what it needs to sell. Marketing thinks sales reps are lazy, and if they just read what was sent to them there would be no problem.

Having conversational themes and points of view that every-one in a company can talk about—through multiple tactical channels and techniques—helps break the stalemate. Internal politics are hard to deal with. But with interesting conversational themes, everyone can stay in their silos and do their thing, while solving the "integrated" problem.

Seven ways to deprogram from a command-and-control attitude

Have you ever walked away from a sales meeting and felt like you were working for a cult? The *rah-rah* about the latest extraordinary product. The motivational speeches about how we can kill the competition. The applause for the new pricing and promotional programs that will reduce sales obstacles. The video set to a great music soundtrack with the last visual frame dissolving to "Now more than ever. The future is ours!"

OK, I may be slightly exaggerating, but if you've been in business for more than a few years, or if you read "Dilbert," you know the feeling.

We get so involved with our own companies—and so fixed on the competition—that it's hard to pull back and get a clear perspective of how we're relating with people on the outside. We pay more and more attention to our company's and direct competitors' plans and less and less to what our customers really want.

It's hard to step back and see the big picture while you're in the trenches, but here are seven ways to deprogram from the all-about-us command-and-control mentality. (Or, as the cult deprogrammers like to say, here's how to do exit counseling.)

1. Undergo the company/competitor immersion treatment

The purpose of this exercise is to show command-and-control traditionalists, especially those who aren't convinced of the need to change marketing practices, just how boring and uninspiring so much conventional all-about-the product-and-us marketing is.

Gather up the sales collateral, press releases, sales presentations, and Web site copy from the company and from the three top competitors and assign the naysayer to do nothing but study these materials for two days. At the end of the second day, ask the person to do the following simple exercise:

* In one simple sentence, how would you say each company is different?
* How would you start a conversation about each of the companies while having coffee with the CEO of an important sales prospect?

Almost always the naysayer realizes that the companies lack points of view worth talking about, and that conventional corporate-speak says nothing more than more of the same. The materials neither help people understand anything new nor inspire them to want to learn more.

After two days, most people are deprogrammed and ready to change. They usually say, "Don't ever make me have to read that drivel again. It was torturous."

Deprogramming people so they think from the customer's point of view instead of the company's is akin to something the late Margaret Singer, a psychology professor at University of California-Berkeley and an expert in cult mind control, once said about religious cult deprogramming, "Getting into the cult consists of the cult recruiter getting the new initiate to *stop* the thought processes, to think only in cult terms and concepts, to give them a narrow frame of thought. The deprogramming process is more a *freeing up* of the person to once again use their mind and to reflect and think and reason and trust their own experience."[3] Free up your mind so that you can connect with the mind-sets of your customers.

2. Delete the adjectives

Another small deprogramming technique is to put a moratorium on the use of adjectives in marketing and sales communications. This isn't a writing exercise. Rather, it's a way to force people to explain what they mean in a more plainspoken and direct way. It gets them to explain instead of proclaim and to teach versus preach.

If the sales presentation starts with, "We have the most vibrant, vital, industry-leading products," but it is now left with, "We have products," the marketer is forced to explain the value of the company in a new way. Instead of using adjectives to describe your product, open with a description of your company's beliefs.

3. Ask new questions

Often when sales slump or campaigns produce sluggish results, we tend to ask, "What can we do?" Instead, ask questions that help better understand why customers are not interested. When Eric Utne, founder of the *Utne Reader*, used this one question, it evoked meaningful three-hour discussions: "What have you been thinking and obsessing about lately?"[4]

By understanding what customers are thinking and obsessing about, it's easier to contribute to the conversation.

4. Think rapport-like vs. report-like

Deborah Tannen, Georgetown University linguistics professor and author of the best-selling books *You Just Don't Understand* and *Talking 9 to 5*, believes that men are more comfortable with report-like talking, and women with rapport-like conversations. Report-like talking reinforces a command-and-control attitude, while rapport-like fosters relationships.

"For most women," says Tannen in *You Just Don't Understand*, "the language of conversations is a way of establishing connections and negotiating relationships. For most men, talk is primarily a means to preserve independence and negotiate and maintain status. . . . From childhood, men learn to use talking as a way to get and keep attention."[5]

So if creating and deepening relationships is a marketing objective, marketing communications should focus more on establishing rapport, and less on reporting data. That means:

* Asking more questions versus giving more statements
* Being other focused versus exclusively me/us focused
* Creating understanding versus attracting attention

5. View marketing as a voice of "customer service," not production

Former high-tech CEO Lou Piazza believes that executives should think of marketing as a service, helping external audiences *and* internal staff. This service mind-set means:

* Internally, bringing customers' views back *into* the company; advising product development, communications, and customer service on how to develop approaches that will improve the customers' experience with the company.
* Helping external influencers such as journalists or analysts understand the market issues and competitive environment, not just those of your company. Note: This is a meaning-making technique that involves first providing context and then talking about how the company's strategy is relevant within that context.

"Typical marketing starts from inside the company and then tries to reach across sales and to the customer. That's why so many marketers are pushing the company's messages against a brick wall," Piazza explains. "I think the much more effective marketing approach is starting from the customer and sales perspective and reaching *into* the company. Because the given isn't the company. The given is the customers."

In other words, a more valuable role for marketers is to communicate customers' needs to people inside the company so that they know what to do differently to provide value to customers and to increase sales.

"I would like marketing to be the voice of the customer," says Piazza. "Tell me what I need to do differently in my product development. Tell me what I need to do differently in my marketing communications activities. Tell me what I need to do differently with product partnerships to provide a more compelling solution for the customer."[6]

This type of marketing service doesn't cost anything, really; it involves listening to customers and bringing their insights back into the company. And it takes place on many platforms—in meetings and Webinars, in online customer communities and forums.

Marketing has traditionally been more like a manufacturing operation, producing advertisements, Web sites, brochures, campaigns, and press releases. Reframed as a service, however, marketing gains even more value through the processes of listening, advising, explaining, and teaching.

The concept of friendliness is a key to marketing as a service.

Friendly people and companies listen because they're really interested in what people have to say. They make it easy for people to chat with them. They share what they're hearing about new ideas, what's happening that may be helpful. They like to talk about what they're learning. They don't lecture or promote but converse in the best sense of the word (the word *converse* comes from the Latin *conversare*—"to turn" or "dance together").

They ask questions—and make it easy for others to do the same in a welcoming kind of way. Think about Southwest or Virgin Atlantic versus airlines with a reputation for being unfriendly. Think about a warm and friendly Whole Foods versus a dingy, overlit convenience store.

A helpful exercise is to rewrite the marketing organization's mission, borrowing from missions of actual customer service organizations. Here are some actual customer service organizations' missions that could easily be applied to marketing:

* Customers should be valued as people and shown courteous and concerned attention to their needs.
* We will provide services "for" and not "to" our customers.
* The customer deserves value.
* Customers deserve honest communication.
* The service process should make sense.

What might it mean to reframe marketing as a customer service function? Here are behaviors associated with delivering customer service from the Office of Human Services at University of California, Berkeley. Most of these behaviors could be applied to how marketers think about their roles.

Care and Respect

❏ Demonstrate a willingness to help.
❏ Listen for customer's knowledge and emotional place.
❏ Try to understand customer's point of view.

Integrity

❏ Response should be genuine, not phony.
❏ Explain reality.
❏ If you can't do something right away, say so.

Accuracy and Thoroughness

- ❏ Make it your responsibility to be the knowledge expert.
- ❏ Be sure that all information you give out is accurate and complete.
- ❏ Summarize discussion to ensure mutual understanding.
- ❏ Identify the real issue and what service is really needed.
- ❏ Use clear, simple language that is easily understood (avoid jargon).

Harmony and Unity

- ❏ Use good listening skills; do not interrupt.
- ❏ Be sensitive to emotional reactions.
- ❏ Be flexible; don't make assumptions.
- ❏ Communicate with a constructive mind.
- ❏ Follow through on actions.

Teamwork

- ❏ Encourage participation by everyone.
- ❏ Be open to ideas different from your own, regardless of the source.
- ❏ Use a variety of methods to solicit input.
- ❏ Look for opportunities to pull in other units to get differing perspectives.

6. *Think of marketing as teaching: Lessons from educational reformer Dennis Littky*

Another way to shift from the command-and-control mind-set is to approach marketing as teaching.

Like teaching, the goal of marketing is not to assert conclusions, but to engage people in a dialogue that leads them to their own conclusions. Teaching and marketing are other-focused. Take, for instance, noted educational reformer Dennis

Littky, cofounder of the Met Schools for inner-city high school students.

In speaking to executives at a conference on business innovation,[7] Littky explained that when he and his colleague Elliot Washor started the first Met School in Providence in 1996, he did not ask, "How can we fix what's wrong with high schools?" Nor did he ask, "How do we fix schools?" Instead, he asked, "Why don't kids like school—and how can we fix *that*?" He talked with students and asked them what would make a difference to them.

Similarly, if we as marketers want to understand how to provide more value, we need to spend less time trying to fine-tune our tactics and more time listening to customers.

Littky found that most kids think school is boring, boring, boring—the same thing consumers say about many marketing programs. They hated sitting in classes and being lectured at all day. That's why they were dropping out. So, the Met eliminated required classes, tests, and grades. Today, instead of a traditional curriculum, each Met student works with an adviser to put together an individualized curriculum based on his or her interests.

The Met's attendance and graduation rates hover near 94 percent—among the best in the state; the school has a 100 percent college acceptance rate, including to top-rated schools such as Brown University and the University of Chicago. Many Met students are the first in their families to go to college. That's not bad for a school whose student body is generally poor—65 percent qualify for federal meal subsidies—and is heavily weighted toward minorities, with 42 percent of the student body Hispanic and 31 percent African-American.

The Met involves students in education, giving kids a say in how to make school decidedly not boring.

Giving customers a say, like the Met does with students, is an especially valuable marketing approach.

7. Empower customers like employees

Diane Hessan, CEO of Communispace and coauthor of *Customer Centered Growth,* told me she believes that marketers can learn how to engage customers from two of the hottest words in business in the past twenty years: *leadership* and *empowerment.*

Management research shows empowered employees deliver better results than employees who feel uninvolved or disengaged. The same "involvement concept," said Hessan, applies to companies' relationships with customers.

Hessan says the following four principles apply to both employee involvement and customer involvement:[8]

1. *Authenticity.* You can't fake it. Your company has to want to involve and listen to customers. "Companies must be prepared not just to *listen* to what customers are saying but to *act* on what they hear," said Hessan.

2. *Ongoing two-way conversation.* Developing trusted relationships requires conversation; it can't be done by one-way communications dissemination. "The quality of the conversation signals to employees and customers that they are truly engaged and involved," notes Hessan. "How many people will speak their minds and get involved if they feel their ideas are going nowhere? Or if no one responds to their suggestions? Not many."

3. *Boundaries need to be clear and mutually accepted.* Involvement doesn't mean that leaders or marketers don't lead. You can't act on all the recommendations from employees or

customers. It's important, advises Hessan, to establish ground rules and boundaries for the engagement process. "Once companies understand that engagement requires conversation—and that these conversations have to be authentic and sincere—then they need to look at how mutual expectations are established between the company and its customers. There needs to be a structure to the dialogue and engagement. Who will participate? How is participation facilitated? What, if any, restrictions are placed on the conversations? Such expectations will likely change over time, as the company and its customers get more comfortable with the process."

4. *Involving people is not a short-term tactic.* Jack Welch observed that one of the surest ways to destroy any employee involvement initiative was to give up on it too quickly. The same applies to involving customers. "Engaging customers is not something you do once in a while, it needs to be a continuous process built into your organizational DNA," according to Hessan. "People today expect to be more involved, and they are skeptical and suspicious. They watch the leader's every move, waiting for a sign that the involvement isn't genuine or their opinions don't really count. So, expect engagement to be a journey, not a one-shot event."

The upside of losing control

In the world of marketing, control is no longer possible. And that's good news for marketers, because now we can redefine a more valuable role for ourselves. That role is talking *with* customers—about what *they* want. In doing so, we're better able to:

* Bring customer ideas *into* the company, which helps research and development (R&D) develop the type of products customers really want. As high-tech CEO Lou Piazza explains, "The given is the customer. Not the company. Marketing is only there to accelerate sales."[9]

* Improve customer satisfaction because we're delivering products customers have told us they want and we've developed the relationships that make customers feel confident in choosing us.

* Shorten decision cycles because we're focused more on helping customers understand and less on promoting to them.

* Find shared points of view that different marketing functions can incorporate into their programs. Although our program tactics may differ, our overall vision can be the same.

* Create more innovative, creative organizations. Dr. Alan Stewart, who has studied the attributes of "conversing companies,"[10] says that in such an environment people:

    - Interact with curiosity, rather than telling in mind
    - Build ideas together, with enthusiasm
    - "Talk up" issues, rather than trying to score points or to persuade
    - Harness the collective intelligence of the group
    - Notice and honor the emotional underpinnings of others' and of our own responses
    - Recognize that right and wrong, winning and losing are irrelevant
    - Welcome diversity of opinion as a wellspring of creativity
    - Sustain openness to creativity

- Appreciate the value of alliances based on interdependency
- Enlarge their vision
- Recognize and acknowledge blind spots in their own perspectives without losing face

Chapter 8 explains how to bring conversational marketing to life through programs, people, and new skills.

Chapter 8

Building a "talk" culture

Marketers are always tweaking their organizations, trying to figure out whether the right people are in the right roles. The last time the Marketing Leadership Council polled its members about organizational structure, two thirds of the marketers said they were dissatisfied with how they were structured. Now along comes conversational marketing with points of view, podcasts, customer communities, and word-of-mouth marketing to further complicate questions about what a marketing organization should look like.

"If you don't help people understand how to institutionalize 'talk' into their organizations, companies aren't going to change all that much," Walter Carl, associate communications professor at Northeastern University, advised me over dinner at the close of the first International Word-of-Mouth Conference in Hamburg, Germany. "Marketers can't just hire a new agency and think that they're done. They have to change internally too."

This chapter offers ideas about:

* How to rethink the marketing organization, morphing traditional roles into eight functions to succeed in conversational marketing: insights, conversational strategy, two-way involvement programs, executive communications, public relations, sales communications, advertising, and technology.
* The responsibilities and skills needed for these eight functions, as well as how to evolve traditional marketing positions, from public relations and research to sales communications and advertising, for these new functions.

Rethink the marketing function: What are the right questions?

Once, the pertinent questions were: Should we be centralized or decentralized? Horizontally focused or industry focused? Product focused or customer focused? (That one always kills me; isn't marketing implicitly suppose to be customer focused?)

Those are "what" questions. Today, it may be better to start from "how" questions when thinking about the marketing organization's design.

* How are we going to create more ways for customers to talk directly with us—and us with them?
* How do customers want to learn about what's new?
* How are we going to stay connected to what people are talking about on blogs, boards, and communities?
* How can we be more effective at meaning-making?
* How can we help people in our company learn how to communicate in new conversational ways?
* How do we use new metrics to analyze what is and isn't working?

Eight important functions for conversational marketing

One way to incorporate these "how" questions and to institutionalize conversations into the culture is to consider the value of the following eight marketing functions:

1. *Insights (a.k.a. "really listening")*—identifying customer habits, market trends, and competitive insights through quantitative research and secondary techniques such as listening to customers, looking at online communities, and reading blogs. *Evolves from traditional market research and competitive intelligence.*

2. *Conversation strategy*—developing points of view, sound bites, questions, stories, and metaphors to be used in marketing, sales, and corporate communications. *Evolves from branding, messaging, account planning, and corporate communications.*

3. *Two-way involvement programs*—creating customer salons, online customer communities, word-of-mouth marketing, blogs, and Webinars. *Evolves from digital marketing, events, and guerrilla marketing.*

4. *Executive communications*—helping executives adopt conversational ideas, styles, and techniques. Some leaders need coaching to move from command-and-control to involve-and-listen. *Evolves from messaging, speech writing, media, and presentation training.*

5. *Public relations*—engaging *with* important influencers and using beliefs to engage them in new conversations. *Puts* *different emphasis on traditional public relations, more two-way conversations as part of influencer outreach, media relations; adds "talkable" point of view ideas to basics.*

6. *Sales communications*—incorporating insights and conversational ideas for sales reps to use with customers; gathering stories from customers and sales reps and feeding them back into the organization. *Evolves from messaging, sales support, marketing communications; more about two-way communications and conversation ideas than producing materials and PowerPoint decks.*

7. *Advertising*—creating advertising approaches that engage and activate people. *Changes emphasis; advertising isn't just the ad; advertising triggers involvement or word of mouth.*

8. *Technology*—shaping strategy, product development, creative programs, and processes by innovatively using technology. *Technology evolves from support function to strategic asset for marketing.*

Insights: Seeing new possibilities

One of the worst things anyone can say to a CEO is, "You're out of touch with your customers." Being out of touch with customers implies that the executive isn't running the business correctly. How can a company provide value to customers if it doesn't really know the customers?

Yet, in our data-driven world, we sometimes confuse research (a process) with insights (an outcome). Data report on what is. Insights are glimpses at what might be, based on the data and on

New Functions, New Competencies

Function	Traditional Role	New Competencies
Insights	Market research Competitive intelligence	Conversation monitoring and analysis Community facilitation and involvement Trend and idea spotting Macro conceptual analysis Ethnography Interviewing and observation expertise (Learning vs. questioning)
Conversation strategy	Branding Messaging Corporate communications/ PR creative account planning	Point-of-view development Linguistic skills Storytelling expertise Conversational writing skills Coaching skills
Two-way involvement programs	Digital marketing/interactive marketing Events	Listening Digital communications skills Broadcast "talk show" skills Participatory event planning skills
Executive communications	Messaging Speech writing Media and speech training	Storytelling expertise Writing to be said Advisory and coaching skills
Public relations	Messaging Media relations Writing Influencer outreach	Two-way involvement approaches Broadcasting skills Relationship building, influence Storytelling expertise Conversational writing skills Faster response, more proactive
Sales communications	Messaging Developing sales support materials	Field sales experience Liaison with insights Creating new ways to involve customers, prospects in conversations
Advertising	Creative Production Media buying	Creating short films vs. "ads" Creative ways to involve customers in brand experience
Technology	Measurement analytics Web skills Production and execution technology skills	Marketing chief information officer, helping to shape marketing strategy, operations, program execution

listening to the market in new ways, observing new patterns, and understanding the implications of those patterns to business strategy.

"You're out of touch with your customers" usually occurs because of too much reporting data and not enough actionable insights to shape strategy.

The late management guru Peter Drucker wrote a great deal about the importance of going outside a company and its existing customers, as that data "tells us only about the current business. They inform and direct tactics."

"For strategy, we need organized information about the environment," Drucker wrote in *On the Profession of Management.* "Strategy has to be based on information about markets, customers and noncustomers; about technology in one's own industry and others; about worldwide finance; and about the changing world economy."[1]

Many customer insights organizations are run by market-research professionals, some of whom have the competencies to take on the challenge while others do not. Those who don't must expand from a process mentality to an outcome mentality. They need to become observers of emerging macro patterns *and* business strategists who can recommend how new insights can be used to shape growth strategies. They have to be adept not only at researching hypotheses but at developing new hypotheses. Internal insights groups are valuable because they help organizations identify and act on new possibilities ahead of the competition.

I've heard people suggest that the insights director should report to the CEO or strategic planning director rather than the CMO, because CMOs are too often wrapped up in tactics. I'd suggest that CMOs delegate more tactical responsibilities and not miss the opportunity to own insights.

Here's an overview of the functions in an insights group:

• *Uses scientific quantitative targeting and positioning research* methods to determine the financially optimal target for the product, preemptive positioning, and financially optimal channels.

• *Manages traditional secondary research* including competitive intelligence and focus groups; analyzes customer service activity patterns and manages customer and prospect analytics.

• *Uses blog and digital news aggregation/analysis to discover and monitor* what people are saying about products, trends, and issues relevant to the company. This function should also be responsible for synthesizing and regularly sharing digital conversation roundups with employees, sales, partners, and other people connected to the organization. The greater the organization's grasp of marketing conversations, the better it will be at contributing to those conversations in ways that help achieve its business objectives.

• *Manages online customer communities.* This means making sure that the community activity and discussions are meaningful to customers and the company. Tactically, it includes sharing ideas with customers and asking for ideas, responding to questions and comments, showing customers how the company is using their ideas, and listening to what and how customers are talking to other customers to better understand customer attitudes, beliefs, and styles. In *Communities Dominate Brands*, authors Tomi Ahonen and Alan Moore make the case that "for the rest of this decade at least, the power of communities will continue to grow . . . there will be a vast difference between the most astute organizations that will adjust to the new community-based marketing environment and those that ignore the change."[2]

Last, insights groups also do the type of work done by the account-planning function at many advertising agencies, as well as the more pragmatic elements of ethnography and behavioral sociology. They are keen observers who detect how customers want to be more emotionally involved with our companies, products, and services.

Conversation strategy: Finding points of view and conversational approaches

Many companies want to be more conversational, but quickly run out of ideas.

"Okay. I wrote three blogs, *now* what do I talk about?" an executive recently asked me.

The problem wasn't style or willingness, but the executive didn't really have anything interesting to say. When people get stuck and start groping for something to talk about, it's often a signal that they, or their companies, know less about their customers or industry than they thought. That's one reason for a conversation strategy capability.

The role of the conversation strategy function is three-fold. One is to develop points of view that connect to and support the business, marketing, and sales strategies. The second role is helping people talk about the point of view. This can mean creating new metaphors, finding supporting stories, crafting sound bites, researching supporting data, and developing questions that provoke thinking around the organization's beliefs. The third role is teaching the following six practices to people in the organization, particularly senior executives, business unit leaders, sales reps, public relations managers, and marketing colleagues:

1. How to communicate more conversationally
2. How to have conversations in a sales meeting versus giving a polished presentation
3. How to participate in digital conversations
4. How to listen—really listen
5. How to keep an ear to the ground for stories, language, and metaphors
6. How to flip the communications mind-set from, "I want to tell you all about our company" to "We're seeing three trends emerge that could be very good or very bad in the industry"

Traditionally, branding and corporate communications have been responsible for elements of conversational strategy, such as value propositions and messaging. However, many of the branding and advertising firms seem to be struggling more than the communications professionals to flip to a conversational approach. Branding experts' natural instinct is to define what the brand should represent to customers from the company's perspective.

It is worth remembering that a brand is what customers think it is, not necessarily what the company says it is. And customers are taking an active role in defining what they think the brand should be. "Marketers offer brand ideas to the market, but those ideas don't truly become brands until they are accepted, adopted, and made over afresh as part of the lives of those who use them," explained Harvard Business School professor John Deighton. "Brand meanings and associations arise as a kind of found consensus between what the marketer wants and what the consumer has use for."[3]

The competencies of communications professionals—people who work regularly with the media and with industry analysts—may be most transferable to the conversation strategy areas. Still, many communications experts need to communicate more conversationally and get off the corporate-speak bandwagon. They must learn to go beyond promoting and messaging to help people understand.

Danish organic grocer Aarstiderne is one of just a few companies to have a conversation department, which came about when marketing and customer service merged into one organization. Here's a blog posting from Annette Hartvig Larsen explaining why the company established a conversation department and how it works.

```
Hi:
We have one . . . a Conversations
Department. And it didn't start on a nice
planned background. We had all read the
Cluetrain Manifesto, and were much inspired
by it, but also saw it not working out as
planned at all.
Our customer service was exactly as old-
fashioned as the rest of them and not really
having conversations with anybody, but
struggling to keep the inbox (3,000 e-mails
a week) down. And we were still a start-up—
only 4 years old!! So we went back to some
of the "methods" we never thought we would
have to use in our "soft" business of deliv-
ering organic vegetables to the doorsteps of
30,000 Danish households a week. We changed
the whole staff of 10 people and moved it
from the province to Copenhagen.
```

Why?

—to hire a staff of actors, students, academics, guides, chefs, etc. (eager to communicate and learn about people and food and to match the customers who are mostly from the city)

—to be able to do short term contracts—only 2 years, then you move on within, or to the next company (no "burnouts" thank you.)

—to start from scratch by de-learning all the bad-corporate habits and introducing the cluetrain-be-yourself-courage (or maybe we hired people who didn't have them?)

—to start up an uncensored forum on the Web site and know that there were people able to answer everything (that one was tough, everybody "hears" everything on a forum!)

—to get closer to our goal of being a transparent company (should be nothing to hide in vegetables and farming?! we ran an Open Space on transparency and one on conversations, including all 100 employees).

Did it work? So far we think so! The Conversations Department is a fun and tough place to work, everybody's engaged, conscious and very responsible (that's often the result of giving freedom.. ;-)), inbox is kept empty and the customers have access to us, meet a human voice and get an honest answer (uh, it hurts some times).

Bottom line for us I guess is: Hire people who really want to do conversations, insist on it when you sooner or later are tempted

```
to compromise . . . and yes management must
be in on it, it's part of a culture they
have to lead!
And this task will never be done and we're
constantly challenged by customers and by
ourselves. It's sort of a hard-fun-thing
doing business this way, but we certainly
don't want to go back and it probably keeps
us in the right colour of water. :-)
Long story—hope it's useful to someone.
Best; Annette, managing director of Aarstiderne
(the seasons)
http://www.aarstiderne.com
```

Two-way involvement programs: Creating conversation channels

The purpose of managing two-way involvement programs is to create channels for conversations, such as blogs, customer communities, town hall meetings, podcasts, customer salons, conferences, and Webinars.

Want to show that products and services are "world-class, vital, revolutionary, and transformational?" Make the top product developers, or the R&D chief, the CEO, or your best customer available for live call-in sessions where interested customers and prospects can "Ask the Experts." Give away advice, offer help, and address customers' biggest concerns. They'll appreciate you for it. Then record each session and offer them as podcasts or as re-broadcast programs from the company's Web site.

Want to be known as a thought leader on a particular topic? Write a blog providing advice, ideas, and observations. And respond personally to people who post talk-back comments.

Go a step further and create debate teams around an industry topic. Have the teams face off at the next big industry conference and let the audience keep score. This type of involvement is much more interesting than the usual forty-minute presentation followed by a lame question-and-answer session.

Want to make sure the next new product doesn't bomb? (An astounding 80 percent of new products fail, according to *New Product News.*) Go to the online customer community and talk about product ideas with customers, asking them for advice and input. A consumer products company recently asked its customer community about a new product concept the internal marketing folks thought was a home run. The community's reaction, "We'd rather eat glass than use that product." Millions saved—as well as a few people's jobs.

Want to help noncompetitive customers learn from and help one another? (This also helps you see what's really on their minds.) Organize regional customer gatherings to discuss industry trends and problems; think of it as an informal, intimate salon rather than a "present at you" conference. This isn't a new idea but one that, done right, is appealing and useful to both contributors and the company.

Back in 1727, Benjamin Franklin organized this type of group and it lasted for forty years, later becoming known as the American Philosophical Club. Franklin's Junto, as it was initially called, brought together practical men of different backgrounds who were willing to help one another and the community. Genuine interest in ideas was the heart of the Friday night discussions. All members had to contribute and all were discouraged from talking "overmuch."

Digital marketing professionals and specialized digital marketing agencies are most quickly evolving into marketing involvement managers. Most participate in their own Web conversations through blogging and message boards, and as members of various communities. So they understand both the value of involvement and how it works.

Important competencies mirror those of Franklin and his Junta friends, including conversational communications skills, interviewing skills, intellectual curiosity, creativity, and a genuine passion about networked communications trends and possibilities.

Watch for radio and television producers and on-air talent to move into the corporate world as marketers develop more podcasts, Webinars, and other talk-show-like formats. These professionals know what makes a good story, how to conduct interviews that spark dialogue, and how to get people interested in participating in the conversation. They also know how to:

* Write for the ear, and, in the case of television veterans, use visuals to engage people in the story
* Work fast, quickly responding to changes and feedback
* Focus on success in telling the story in ways people will understand rather than worrying needlessly on perfecting the words, the headline, the visuals, or the narration

Executive communications: Coaching for clarity, understanding, and conversations

Executives' influence on employees, customers, investors, and partners is formidable. When they talk, people listen and make judgments about the company.

If CEO talk is muddled, people may assume that the company's strategy is unclear, that the speaker doesn't really care about the audience, or perhaps that the CEO isn't an especially effective leader. Coaching executives to be effective conversationalists—not speech givers or message deliverers—is hugely important because of these judgments.

In reporting how CEOs' meandering, unintelligible conversations during analyst calls affect stock prices, Landon Thomas of the *New York Times* wrote, "More than ever, investors are holding chief executives accountable for their ability to articulate a clear and compelling vision. . . . A garbled sentence or a muddled articulation of a corporate strategy can not only mar the public profile of a chief executive but also prompt a run on the stock."[4] And it can diminish customer confidence and trust.

Executives' remarks during analyst calls, conference speeches, and sales meetings are increasingly being recorded so that a wider audience can access the remarks after the event. As a result, executives' conversational skills are especially important. They don't need to be Churchillian orators or charismatic characters like Richard Branson or Herb Kelleher, but they do need to be able to convey ideas in clear, interesting, and genuine ways.

Whether the executive communications function should be in marketing or whether it should report directly to the CEO is up for debate. What is not in question is that executive communications needs to be tightly connected with insights and conversational strategy. Those market insights, points of view, and stories are exactly what an executive needs to know to be a more effective conversationalist.

For example, when Chuck Schwab was preparing for a media briefing tour, he went to the Schwab community of high net worth investors and asked them for *their* opinions about the investing climate.

Executive communications' role as adviser and coach to executives is more important than the role of ghostwriter and speechwriter. Executive communications professionals need to work closely with the conversation strategist to shape platform ideas that the executives believe in and like to talk about. They also provide the supporting facts, stories, and sound bites that the CEOs can build into their thinking and conversations.

Executive communications directors must be respected by the executives with whom they work. Otherwise, the executives won't listen to them or heed their advice. The most effective executive communications professionals:

* Understand business, the company, and the market
* Know how to synthesize complex information into concise, clear conversational ideas
* Understand how to coach executives to find a style that is comfortable and genuine, that informs and inspires
* Are intelligent, self-confident, direct, well-read, and know how to push without being pushy

CEOs are more likely to adopt a conversational style when they:

* Talk about ideas and points of view about which they are passionate (this is why I recommend involving them in point-of-view brainstorming workshops)
* Have a chance to talk about points of view during informal conversations with trusted members of their executive teams, getting comfortable with the ideas and taking ownership before going "public"
* Have relevant metaphors, examples, and stories that they can tap into—the more the better
* Focus conversations around no more than three points of view

＊ Are comfortable *not* using business and industry jargon, just plain-speak

Remind the CEO that the purpose of communicating with any group is to help foster understanding, not to preach, tell, sell, or lecture. After an analyst meeting or customer speech, the critique is simply, "Did the executive help people understand that idea? What worked in creating understanding—and what didn't?"

Executives spend up to 80 percent of their day talking, according to research from the Tuck School of Business at Dartmouth College. "Estimates from research conducted at the Tuck School suggest that relative to total work time, the time spent communicating [with constituencies] by CEOs is between 50 and 80 percent, on average, across all CEOs at the Fortune 500 companies."[5]

Many CEOs are natural conversationalists. Most need more insights, ideas, metaphors, and stories to draw from. That's the role of executive communications.

Public relations: Right skills, wrong box?

The role of public relations is either going to expand greatly in this conversational marketing world, or it's going to disappear. It certainly won't stay the same.

Although the concept of public relations is "relating to publics," the function has largely turned into a one-way press release and publicity factory. There's a whole lot of "messaging" for the media, but not much creativity in generating new conversational communications approaches.

Around 1996, when the Web was taking off, I predicted that

public relations would be the profession to lead online communications. After all, the Web wasn't meant to be an online brochure or a Flash advertisement. Who better to manage this new media than public relations professionals? As it turned out, I was wrong.

Public relations mostly stayed in its box, while advertising, direct-response, and new media types took ownership of the Web. Web communications was viewed as a marketing function, not a public relations function because the view was that PR people are just the publicity people.

PR is at another crossroads today as conversational communications channels such as podcasts and blogs come online. The fundamental communications skills of public relations people are especially relevant, but these professionals need to climb out of their media relations and employee communications boxes if they want to expand their roles and their value to the organization. Using technology to automate conventional practices—automatic mailings, publicity monitoring, and competitor quote pickup—won't increase the value of the function. The greater goal is building understanding and relationships.

So far, overall these professionals have been laggards in new digital channels and new digital communications techniques such as digital storytelling or blogging. And, if reading press releases is any evidence, they're some of the worst corporate-speak offenders. (Do real people ever actually say what is in press release quotes?)

Also surprising is that a new cadre of word-of-mouth marketing specialists are taking on word-of-mouth communications, which traditionally had its roots in public relations.

Public relations executives and organizations should consider the following items to become more relevant and add greater value:

* Look at the profession through a new lens, redefining its purpose as helping all the company's "publics" better understand its purpose, positions, and value.
* Hire broadcast journalists to help find stories, tell stories, and help you learn how to write to be said, not write to be read.
* Start a peer-to-peer media relations approach. If a CEO thinks that *Forbes* should be interested in the company, why not have the CEO directly contact a reporter and talk about the idea?
* Learn from Nancy Reagan: Just say no. Public relations people need to push back on internal folks, like product management directors or sales directors who want them to "get press" for ideas that aren't press-worthy. Instead, suggest alternative ways to help the right people, such as customers or reviewers, learn about the products. You know what reporters are interested in; you are not failing if you refuse to push a bad idea on someone who doesn't want it.
* Become story gatherers versus case study writers: take on the responsibility for finding and telling interesting customer stories. The stories shouldn't be conventional case study exhortations about all the benefits the customer realized from using your product, but rather slices of what happened that were especially surprising, unconventional, or rewarding.
* Get to know the people who influence your customers, and build relationships with them. Some may be journalists and writers; others are likely to be consultants, analysts, association executives, academics in your field, and large companies that affect industry practices.

* Take back word-of-mouth marketing.
* Hang out with the insights people.

Sales communications: Beyond product collateral and PowerPoint decks

Dave, a top-performing sales rep of a large global consulting firm, told me that he constantly scans articles, clips out interesting stories, and sends them via overnight mail to prospects with a $10 bill and a note that basically says, "Thought you'd be interested in this. Can we meet next week for coffee to talk more about what it might mean to your business?" (The $10 is for the coffee.)

Dave makes six figures as a sales executive. So why is he monitoring news in order to have something to talk about with prospects? Imagine the thousands of Daves doing the same sort of monitoring every day. Should Dave being doing this? Or should sales support? The answer is somebody needs to own it because sales reps are always looking for new ideas to talk about with prospects. If sales reps don't get ideas from marketing or sales support, they use their own time to find the ideas. They know they need something interesting to talk about to get a meeting with a prospect.

Sales executives of a large software company told me that customers want to talk about new trends and insights in their vertical industries, but most of the information they get from marketing is about new product features and benefits—nothing that gives them a reason to meet with a client to talk about new ideas.

Sales representatives are crying out for fresh new things to talk about.

The role of sales communications is to work with the conversational strategy to:

* Provide the points of view, stories, and anecdotes to sales reps
* Coach sales executives on how to engage customers in conversations around the points of view
* Learn what is and isn't working in sales and how sales communications can help improve the sales process
* Continue to provide valuable competitive intelligence, product, pricing, and service information
* Listen closely to sales reps and customers for interesting views, stories, and language that can be shared with others in the company

The role of adviser and coach is particularly important. Most sales-oriented organizations still think that the primary job of sales support is talking about the product and company, instead of helping sales reps find ways to engage in conversations that build relationships and help them better understand the prospects' real issues.

For example, EMC, the $8.2 billion storage systems company, recently posted a job opening on Monster.com for a senior-level principal marketing program manager to work as a liaison between product marketing and field sales. Some of the criteria recognize the need for two-way conversations, while others show how rooted companies are in pushing their product messages. Here are some excerpts from the posting. Note that the second bullet is the old, rather unrealistic push approach, while the third begins to recognize the need for conversations beyond product:

* "Responsibilities: advisory-level member of the team within Field Marketing that focus on Products and Services or Core Messages for Enterprise, Commercial, and/or partners"

* "Create, develop, version, and integrate EMC product and core messages and content for customers, partners, and internal audiences worldwide"
* "Initiate strategy discussions with customers and go beyond knowledge transfer to influence/change customer perspectives and buying criteria"
* "Develop sales positioning for field use in one-on-one discussions with customers, to take them from zero to compelling in minutes"

Most sales reps, particularly those selling complex products or services, know that you can't build understanding from zero to compelling in a few minutes. Deals happen based on many conversations about the customer's needs, how the company's products can address those needs, and about beliefs that help the prospect feel confident in the company's ability to provide more value than its competitors.

The best competence for someone running sales communications is field sales experience. It's difficult for marketing people who have never sold to understand the relationship-building process in selling, the types of information and ideas needed to support different selling situations, and different phases of the deal development relationship.

The other important competences include:

♦ *The ability to analyze emerging trends, insights, and company strategies*—and to know what it means to customers; this includes framing the information within the customer's context and showing what's most relevant to them.

♦ *Strong oral and communications skills.* Straight talk, plain-speak communications skills include the ability to listen, synthesize complex information, and communicate it clearly without overly simplifying it. The best sales communications professional doesn't have a PowerPoint addiction; he or she helps sales reps talk about ideas.

+ ***The willingness to get dirty.*** By this, I mean the willingness to go out on sales calls and talk—really talk—to customers.

Advertising: Talk about creative

The best advertising engages and activates us to do something more—pass the ad around to friends because it's so fresh and funny; click on links to learn more; tack a print ad to our bulletin board so it stays fresh in our mind.

Not long ago, a friend e-mailed me a link to the new Honda Civic ad where a chorus sings and hums the sounds of the new Civic—zooming down the highway, opening the sunroof, driving over cobblestones, screeching around a tight corner—as the video shows the car in action. Every few seconds the camera pans to the people in the chorus "singing" the car sounds. Very cool.

So cool that in one week alone almost one million people went to the Honda site to watch the Civic "choir" ad. That's right. One week, almost a million people, and it was virtually free media for Honda. Why? Because the folks who created the ad found a visually and aurally compelling way to involve consumers. More important, unlike so many of the car ads running on television today, this one highlighted the automobile's features: speed, reliable shocks, great handling. The Civic choir ad represented a great balance between substance and style.

Similarly, Sony released its Bravia commercial over the Web

and millions clicked to watch the small movie capturing the sight of 250,000 multicolored super balls bouncing down the streets of San Francisco, set against the beautiful soundtrack of José Gonzalez's song "Heartbeat."

Advertising isn't dead, but it's evolving from yakking at us to involving us. We don't want to be interrupted by it, but if the content is engaging, we will choose to watch it, maybe even send it to others.

We'll choose to see ads through many more channels than television or print, most notably online, on our mobile phones, or on our portable music devices. But the advertising has to help us in some way—inform us about something we want to know. For example, a text message stating that cashmere sweaters at Saks are going on sale tomorrow. Or, it should entertain us, like the Bravia and Civic ads.

Advertising will need more creative short filmmakers; copywriters who can capture an idea that is succinct enough for the smallest mobile phone screen; product designers who know how to turn the product into the ad (think creative packaging); and creative conceptualists who understand how to involve people in the advertising experience. The creative has to be so good that people choose to be involved.

Technology: Elevating the marketing chief information officer

Marketing has evolved into a new trinity: strategy, conversations, and technology. That's why every marketing organization needs its own chief information officer.

Technology has created the channels for direct dialogue between consumers and companies, allowing us to connect and converse with customers and prospects all over the world. Technology has automated marketing functions, customer search, and information-gathering approaches, behavioral and search-specific advertising techniques, and research and insight-monitoring techniques. Technology has opened up a new world of collaborative, participatory ways to learn, market, and buy. And there are many more changes coming.

The chief information officer needs a seat at the table to help shape strategy; creative, conversational approaches; analytics; process streamlining; and idea development.

In addition to a strategic technology leader, marketing organizations need technologists who have the skills to produce programs in cost-effective ways, who know how to use technology to pinpoint the information preference and behavioral patterns of target customers and who can tap into the many, many emerging digital channels.

Rituals: New ways of working to build conversations into the organizational culture

Here are a few approaches that can help people begin to build conversational marketing practices into the organization's everyday operations.

1. Require digital stories at annual or quarterly planning meetings and as part of new product plans

Rather than PowerPoint presentations, use digital stories to kick off new product introductions, sales campaigns, or change programs. Require small teams of two to three people to produce a two-minute digital story (with voiceover, images, and a soundtrack) about why they think a new product, program, or acquisition is especially valuable or relevant. The storytelling format forces people to tell, not show. Rather than present a bunch of data, a good storyteller finds what's most relevant among all the benefits, writes down what she'll say, uses images to help convey ideas, speaks in the first person using everyday plain-speak, and taps into genuine beliefs. Discussions about different teams' stories, as well as their points of view, will help all team members more fully understand the value of the new product, the program, or the plan. Also, the digital stories themselves lay a foundation for communications and advertisings programs.

2. Rethink your hiring and orientation processes

Start changing job descriptions, interviewing approaches, and hiring processes to find talent that understands conversational marketing *and* has conversational marketing competencies. Create new interviewing guides to probe candidates' conversational marketing skills. Some qualities to look for include the following:

* Intellectual curiosity, interested in ideas and people beyond those in the company or industry; involved with and understands new conversational channels, like social networks
* Voracious readers and observers
* Ability to cut to the core of an issue or situation and diagnose causes of the problem
* Creative thinking; ability to develop pragmatic ways to solve problems
* Outstanding oral and written communications skills, including listening skills
* Perspective and an ability to focus on what matters most to achieving the right outcomes; focusing on success versus perfection; knowing when to cut losing initiatives

* Confidence and self-esteem
* Fearlessness
* Collaborative approach to work: open to other people's ideas, prefers to work with a galaxy of talented people rather than being the star
* A sense of humor and playfulness; we all still have the minds of our five-year-old selves
* Ability to stay above the fray to see the big picture and emerging patterns; an astute observer, if you will

"One of the reasons many people fail to fully appreciate what's changing is that they're down at the ground level, lost in a thicket of confusing, conflicting data," says Gary Hamel, founder of Strategos and visiting professor of strategic and international management at the London Business School. "You have to make time to step back and ask yourself, 'What's the big story that cuts across all these little facts?' "[6]

One way to probe a candidate's conversational marketing competencies is to ask him to come to one of the interviews prepared to talk about his point of view on marketing or the company's industry. This helps to assess the candidate's knowledge—and his interest in the job because of the homework he'll need to do. And the conversation about his point of view will provide insights into how well he thinks, listens, and asks questions. It also helps to see how comfortable he is during conversations. Is he open to other people's views—or does he adamantly defend his perspective and remain closed to their opinions?

For orientation, share stories and lore about the company, explain the thinking behind the company's point of view, set up orientation programs where new marketing people immediately meet with sales reps, customers, and all the "other" audiences that are so important to a marketing person's success.

3. Walk the talk

At every monthly or quarterly planning meeting, make sure the agenda reflects new conversational marketing practices, such as:

* What are we hearing from customers?
* What are the three most surprising insights from our customer communities?
* What new topic is the market beginning to talk about and why?
* How can we talk about our point of view in new ways this quarter?
* What should we add to our Nine Block Conversation Planner this quarter?
* What are the most interesting new patterns we're seeing?
* How are the new stories we've been hearing relevant to our ongoing conversations with customers?

Recognize and reward people who are trying new approaches—listening, involving customers, using straight talk, finding interesting new points of view, and uncovering new stories.

Swap out people who can't make the adjustment. Show that to succeed in the organization, you must be willing to learn and adapt to the right new skills.

4. Bring in more outside talent

The fastest way to force organizational change is to bring in outside talent specialized in these new conversational marketing approaches. This external talent will help you adopt new practices more quickly, help train your internal people, and introduce new energy and passion.

5. Use your training budget to develop conversational marketing skills

Use your training budget to create a conversational marketing boot-camp program for everyone in the marketing organization. Some training programs to consider include the following:

* Uncovering and using points of view
* Digital storytelling
* New "write to speak" writing skills
* Online customer community management and facilitation
* How to listen, really listen
* Cultivating conversations as a core marketing process
* Creating online salons
* How to see emerging marketing patterns using techniques like situational awareness mapping, consumer-generated media analysis, and customer data analytics

Conversational marketing isn't a revolution, it's an evolution. Many existing marketing skills and practices are quite relevant. Most marketing roles need to be changed approximately 45 degrees, eliminating some practices, adding others. All need to be viewed through the lens of the customer: What do customers want to know and how do *they* want to be involved with your company? If you invite customers in and open up the dialogue, they will show you what needs to be done. (Or not.)

Last, rather than asking, "What should we be doing?" or "What is the right organizational structure?" focus on how to do things in new ways. Marketing's role is to find new ways to better understand customers and to help customers understand our companies in ways that are interesting to them.

Chapter 9

Be more interesting—conversations, passion, and an honest point of view

Two events that happened within the same two weeks show the far left and far right of conversational marketing. One demonstrated just how much people want to have a say and what they'll do to provoke conversation. The other highlighted how the "learned lectures" communications approach falls flat, even for the most intelligent, articulate people.

Michael Esordi, a graphic artist living in Connecticut, decided to sell his soul, auctioning it off on eBay, another first for the online bidding site. My first thought was, "What's up with this guy? Is he some kind of religious nut?"

After a little digging, it became clear that Esordi's real purpose was to provoke discussion and get more people thinking about spirituality. "Behind the seller of a soul is simply a smoke screen," wrote *Providence Journal* reporter Bryan Rourke, who interviewed the soul seller. "What Esordi really wants is to be a provocateur of public discourse."

"My idea is to put the idea out there and step back," Esordi told Rourke. "It gets people to think and maybe believe in something. Souls are sold in small and large ways every day. Often, it's something that happens little by little, almost unconsciously because we've become inured."[1]

In other words, Esordi's point of view was that we take our souls for granted and perhaps we shouldn't.

Esordi created a framed certificate of his soul, a piece of expressionist art work if you will. It reads: "The Soul. Does it exist? What is it worth? Can it be sold?" In addition to the certificate, Esordi created a Web site, www.canitbesouled.com, where the highest bidder could explain the reason for buying the certificate for a soul.

This soul selling shows just how much people want to have a say and how far they are willing to go to provoke dialogue and get more people talking about ideas they see as meaningful.

When the auction ended, forty-eight people had bid on Esordi's soul. The certificate sold for $65.

Learned lectures fail to connect

As one soul was auctioned off, another was honored when mourners gathered to pay their respects to Coretta Scott King at her funeral in Atlanta. More than three dozen people spoke at the service including President George W. Bush, the Reverend Jesse Jackson, poet Maya Angelou, former presidents Jimmy Carter and Bill Clinton, and Senator Hillary Rodham Clinton.

Bill Clinton gave an inspiring, emotionally charged, off-the-cuff speech, peppered with one-liners that the audience boisterously applauded, including "You want to treat our friend Coretta like a role model? Then model her behavior."

According to many observers, Senator Clinton's remarks were more formal than her husband's, delivered in a measured, restrained, and deliberate style. The contrast between the two Clintons was vivid, as was the audience's reaction. They welcomed Bill like a returning hero, while they respectfully listened to Hillary.

"I think Bill Clinton delivers inspiring addresses," explained Theodore C. Sorensen, one of John F. Kennedy's best-known speechwriters. "Hillary is more likely to deliver learned lectures."[2]

A few years back, I had lunch with the late MIT professor Michael Dertouzos who had just returned from the World Economic Forum in Davos, Switzerland, where he had heard Mrs. Clinton speak. "She was absolutely brilliant," he said. "Her understanding of complex issues and her ability to get up and talk about those issues was remarkable. I don't think anyone else at Davos came close to her in being able to articulate such cogent perspectives on today's social, political, and economic issues."

Yet, because Mrs. Clinton speaks formally, in full paragraphs and with little emotion, it's often difficult to see things from her point of view and to connect with her as a person. Like many CEOs and marketing programs, Mrs. Clinton's knowledge is substantive, but because her style lacks emotion and the language of conversations, it often fails to move us.

"It is telling that during her 2000 Senate campaign, Mrs. Clinton's advisers were struck by her tendency to speak in perfect paragraphs," wrote *New York Times* reporter Raymond Hernandez about the differences between the Clintons' communications style. "In the end, they urged her to use the kind of sound bites that would be easier to digest."[3]

To succeed in a conversational world, marketers (much like Hillary Clinton) need to reset our style so people can more easily understand our points—and get who we are as people. Although we may be interested about certain ideas and want to tell everyone everything, no one is likely to be interested in everything we might want to tell them.

McDonald's provokes meaningful conversations about McJobs

Conversational marketing doesn't just inform and tell, but in true meaning-making style it is relevant, frames ideas within existing contexts, shows patterns, and, most important, creates an emotional connection with the people.

McDonald's is a company that largely understands how to do this. CEO Jim Skinner recognizes the need to talk with people—customers, community members, shareholders, and employees—all the time, especially about highly relevant and potentially controversial issues. "Business is like life. We are never finished. The dialogue continues as it should because we continue to listen to our stakeholders and adapt to the evolving changes of the world in which we live."[4]

When Merriam-Webster's *Collegiate Dictionary* released its 2003 edition with the term "McJob," defined as a low paying and dead-end job, McDonald's challenged that assumption and opened up a highly public discussion about the fast-food company and its employment practices. (Note that challenging assumptions is one of the nine things people like to talk about.)

In a letter to Merriam-Webster, McDonald's then-CEO Jim Cantalupo said the term was "an inaccurate description of restaurant employment" and "a slap in the face to the 12 million men and women who work in the restaurant industry. More than one thousand of the men and women who own and operate McDonald's restaurants today got their start by serving customers behind the counter."[5] McDonald's also e-mailed the letter to the media and has continued to publicly challenge assumptions and engage in conversations about the topic, using all of the principles of meaning making.

At the 2005 Business for Social Responsibility Conference, Skinner provided context around the issue. "Three of our seven CEOs, including me, started as restaurant crew members at McDonald's as did nearly half of our top fifty executives in the organization today. There are tens of thousands of stories about opportunity I could tell you. Like Jan Fields who joined us as a young mother working her way through college in 1977, and today is president of one of our U.S. divisions, managing 4,400 restaurants in twenty-four states with annual sales of $8.2 billion."

He also explained why the topic is relevant. "We took this debate worldwide because in many of our countries, a job at McDonald's is a highly coveted position. We realized that those of us that provide jobs which serve as a springboard to successful careers need to stress the opportunities we provide, the value of first jobs, the value of training and experience, and the value of achieving advancement through hard work."[6]

One last note: When you listen to Skinner talk about this issue, his passion draws you into the discussion. The emotion behind the words turns information into meaning.

Attract interest, create understanding, build trust

Marketing is about being interested enough to attract interest, creating understanding, and building trust. McDonald's, Sun Microsystems, Women & Infants Hospital, Dove, CEO Lou Piazza, architect Chuck Dietsche, and many of the other companies featured in this book recognize that having something interesting to talk about—something of interest to customers—is a powerful way to engage them.

If people don't trust companies, as the research in Chapter 1 shows, they are less likely to buy our products or services. No matter how much we've invested in product development or how large our marketing budgets or how creative our marketing approaches. James Carville famously remarked during the first Clinton presidential campaign, "It's the economy, stupid." Adapted for us marketers, "It's the customers, stupid."

How do we earn more trust? We can start by doing the following:

* Delivering products and services that provide value to customers.
* Making it easier for people to get to know our companies and feel good about doing business with us. Relationships are based on good product experiences as well as understanding "who" a company is, on both a rational and emotional basis.
* Communicating with honesty, transparency, and good ol' forthrightness. In this hyperconnected world, companies have no control. Information gets out and people talk about our companies all the time. If we want to improve our brand perception or reputation, we have to be more involved in customer conversations and make it easier for people to talk about our companies and products with other people.

By conversing with customers, we begin working *with* them and they with us. We're collaborators working together to create mutual value, instead of opposing teams in an "us-against-them" environment. When you open communication channels and listen, really listen, marketing gets easier because customers *want* to tell us what they want—and what they don't want.

Four steps for creating interesting things to talk about

Points of view exist in every organization, and they are potent ways to jump-start conversations. The first step in finding them is through ear-to-the-ground research, such as:

* Listening to customers in new ways—not for just what they're saying but also for the emotions behind what they're saying.
* Tapping into the beliefs of people within the company. What do people believe that would be interesting to talk about? What industry or issue points of view might help customers make sense of choices?
* Tuning into the market conversation in new ways, using new tools to better understand the big picture context, determining what issues are becoming more or less relevant, and evaluating how people feel about certain topics.

The second step is to put the beliefs and views through the Nine Block Conversation Planner™, which helps to synch the ideas up with the nine topics people most like to talk about: aspirations and beliefs, David versus Goliath, avalanche about to roll, anxieties, counterintuitive/contrarian, personalities, how-to, glitz and glam, and seasonal and event-related.

Third, bring conversations to life by talking (and writing) like a real person talks in all communications, even the written ones. Be casual. Be brief. Be passionate. Make it easy for people to talk back. Create more conversational programs that open up two-way dialogues between customers and people in the company, as well as customers with other customers. Cut back on the one-way all-about-us promotional material. (SAP, the third largest software company in the world, slashed sales collateral and increased its sales.)

Fourth, make sure conversational marketing is someone's job—or incorporated into everyone in marketing's jobs. Hold people accountable for adding points of view into the basic marketing tool kit and reward them for creating multiple ways for everyone inside and outside the company to talk about those ideas in ways that build understanding and meaning.

Figure 9-1 shows how all these steps work together to help marketers move beyond the buzz.

The conversations are the work

Marketing's primary purpose is no longer "producing" things, like ads, press releases, and brochures. The purpose is helping people understand our organizations and products in ways that are meaningful to them. Two overlooked ways to do this are listening to customers and making them feel heard; and making it easy and interesting for people to talk about ideas, issues, and points of view. Through these conversations, people become more involved, and involvement is the prerequisite to action, whether it is making a decision to buy, advocating on an organization's behalf, or just changing a perspective about an issue or product.

Poet David Whyte often speaks to business executives about leadership and change. One of his points of view is that leaders need to help employees feel that they belong, and conversations are an important way to do this. He once remarked, "Leaders' conversations are not about the work, they are the work."[7]

To help bring customers into our companies, we marketers too should realize that marketing conversations are our work.

1 ear-to-the-ground research

Tap into CEO's beliefs   Listen in new ways   Run a point-of-view workshop

Hold a clearness committee   Think more narrowly   Explore new metaphors

Go on a walkabout

PUTTING
BEYOND BUZZ
TOGETHER

points of view

Aspirations and beliefs

    David. vs. Goliath

2   Avalanche about to roll

    Anxieties

    Contrarian/Counterintuitive

Personalities and personal stories

How-to

Glitz and glam

Seasonal/event-related

conversation-worthiness filter **3**

That's interesting. Tell me more.

True	Relevant	Genuine
Fresh	Connects with strategy	Memorable
Talkable	Leggy	Likable

MAKES MEANING • CONTEXT • RELEVANCY • PATTERN MAKING • EMOTION

straight talk style

4 How a real person talks

First person vs. anonymous third person

Sincere and straightforward

What's the point?

Stories. Sound bites. Questions.

Kill the buzzwords, empty adjectives

5 applying to marketing functions
and conversational programs

Figure 9-1.

APPENDIX

The Nine Block Conversation Planner™

Aspirations	David vs. Goliath	Avalanche about to roll
Anxieties	Counterintuitive/ Contrarian	Personalities
How-to	Glitz and Glam	Seasonal/Event-Related

The Conversational Value Formula

| Ideas
Beliefs
Advice
Perspectives | X | Context
Relevance
Patterns
Emotion | X | Counterintuitive
Anxieties
Aspirational
David vs.
Goliath
Personalities
Avalanche
How-to
Glitz & Glam
Event-related | = | Conversational
Value |

What We Believe Questions: An Expanded List

1. We believe that . . .
2. Our take on the situation is that . . .
3. The narrow slice of the issue that more people should understand is . . .
4. The one thing that matters the most in this issue/trend is . . .
5. People are wasting too much time talking about . . .
6. The thing that should worry people is . . .
7. Conventional thinking says this, but we think it's really . . .
8. The area where too much money and time is wasted in this industry is . . .
9. Overcoming this one obstacle would change the game . . .
10. To make a big difference in this area we should focus on just this one thing . . .
11. We never want to be associated with . . .
12. Our product/industry/company matters more/less today because . . .
13. To make customers believers they need to understand this one thing . . .
14. If you had a crystal ball, what changes would you predict for our industry over the next two years?
15. What gets me most excited about our industry/business is . . .
16. What outrages/frustrates people about common practices in our business/field?
17. What makes people anxious about this issue/trend?
18. If we were to look at our business/organization as a cause, what would it be?
19. What most surprises people about this issue?

20. What makes you angry about perceptions of our business/industry?

21. Why is our industry/service especially relevant at this point in time?

22. The biggest risk in this industry is (. . .) and no one wants to talk about it because . . .

23. People would be very surprised if they knew this about our industry/organization . . .

24. The thing that could disintermediate our business/industry is . . .

25. I'm hopeful that one day our industry will . . .

Point-of-View Workshop Checklist

1. Who to invite

   Look for people who are:

   ❏ Knowledgeable about the company, customers, and industry

   ❏ Intellectually curious

   ❏ Open-minded

   ❏ Comfortable with ambiguity and talking about possibilities and concepts

   ❏ Passionate but not zealots

   ❏ Respectful of other people's views and opinions

   ❏ Can put aside their personal agendas for a day

   ❏ Not naysayers or alpha fraidy cats

2. Facilitator qualities

   ❏ Knows your business

   ❏ Understands the outcome to be arrived at

   ❏ Knows how to provoke discussion, question assumptions in ways that open people up to discussion

   ❏ Knows way to get people to contribute vs. just participate

   ❏ Good at summarizing

   ❏ Can flow with and adapt session to the energy of the group

3. Room and materials

   ❏ Off-site location

   ❏ Room with windows

   ❏ Small café tables with no more than four chairs per table

   ❏ Fifteen sticky note pads per table

❏ One pad of plain paper per table with crayons for doodling

❏ One flip chart per table

❏ For facilitator: flip chart easel; three pads of easel paper with adhesive backing, whistle for calling time at end of each speed-thinking session

4. Format

❏ Explain purpose (15 minutes)

❏ Group introductions (15 minutes)

❏ Warm-up: Market trends and context (1.5 hours)

❏ Small group breakout sessions: 100 mile per hour "12 beliefs" sessions (1.5 to 2 hours)

❏ Coming together: What we believe (1.5 to 2 hours)

❏ Wrap: What's the word?

POV Litmus Test

Does it hit at least four of the ten success characteristics?

1. *Is it engaging?* Does it evoke the response, "That's kind of interesting. Tell me more."

2. *Is it true?* Can you support the point of view with facts, trend information, aggregated insights, or other data?

3. *Is it relevant?* The more relevant the idea to the intended audience, the more interested people will be.

4. *Is it genuine?* Do you believe in the idea—truly?

5. *Is it fresh?* Is the view new and different from most conversations around the topic?

6. *Does it connect the dots to your business?* Does it build customer trust? Demonstrate your organization's special expertise in a particularly valuable area to customers? Help people more clearly understand your strategy?

7. *Is it memorable?* Does the view stick in a person's head? Is it easy to remember?

8. *Is it "talkable"?* Is it easy for people to talk about the concept in their own words and tell their own stories around it? Does it jump-start two-way talk?

9. *Is it leggy?* Does the idea resonate with multiple audiences, through multiple communications channels?

10. *Is it likeable?* Do people like talking about the point of view? Is it so inspiring, provocative, brave, or bold that they naturally jump into conversations about it?

Recommended Reading

Albanese, Andrew. *Graduation Day: The Best of America's Commencement Speeches* (New York: William Morrow, 1998).

Brown, Juanita. *The World Café: Shaping Our Futures Through Conversations That Matter* (San Francisco, Calif.: Berrett-Koehler, 2005).

Gardner, Howard. *Leading Minds: An Anatomy of Leadership* (New York: Basic Books, 1995).

Greenleaf, Robert. *The Servant as Leader* (Westfield, Ind.: The Robert Greenleaf Center, 1991).

Jensen, Eric. *Teaching with the Brain in Mind* (Alexandria, Va.: Association for Supervision & Curriculum Development, 1998).

Lakoff, George. *Don't Think of an Elephant* (White River Junction, Vt.: Chelsea Green Publishing, 2004).

Lambert, Joe. *The Digital Storytelling Cookbook and Travelling Companion* (Berkeley, Calif.: Digital Diner Press, 2003).

McKenna, Regis. *Total Access: Giving Customers What They Want in an Anytime, Anywhere World* (Boston: Harvard Business School Press, 2002).

Perlich, Martin. *The Art of the Interview* (Kingston, N.Y.: Empty Press, 2003).

Sandra, Jaida N'Ha, and Jon Spayde. *Salons: The Joy of Conversations* (Gabriola Island, B.C., Canada: New Society Publishers, 2001).

Notes

Chapter 1. Enough with the marketing blah blah blah— let's talk about something interesting

1. John Battelle, "Are You Becoming Irrelevant to Your Customers?" AdAge.com, July 12, 2005.
2. Author interview with Firepond executives, October 2000.
3. Karen Maru File, Ben Judd, and Russ Alan Prince, "Interactive Marketing: The Influence of Participation on Positive Word-of-Mouth and Referrals," *The Journal of Services Marketing,* Fall 1992, pp. 6, 9, 10.
4. David Maister and Lois Kelly, "Marketing Is a Conversation," *New Zealand Lawyer,* February 2006, pp. 7–9.
5. David Einstein, "Novell's Muddy Message," Forbes.com, May 5, 2000.
6. Golin/Harris Trust Survey, 2002.
7. "A Crisis of Confidence: Rebuilding Bonds of Trust," Yankelovich State of Consumer Trust, 2004.
8. As quoted in Bob Garfield's "Listenomics" article, AdAge.com, October 10, 2005.
9. Gary Hart, "Who Will Say 'No More'?" *The Washington Post,* August 24, 2005, p. A15.
10. http://www-306.ibm.com/ebusiness/ondemand/us/innovation/innovation/innovation_flat.shtml, June 24, 2005.

11. Steve Hamm, "Speed Demon: How Smart Companies Are Creating New Products—and Whole New Businesses—Almost Overnight," *Business Week,* March 27, 2006.

Chapter 2. Make meaning, not buzz

1. *Frontline,* "The Age of AIDS: Interview Bono," May 30, 2006; transcript at www.pbs.org/wgbh/pages/frontline/aids/interviews/bono.html.
2. James Traub, "The Statesman," *New York Times Magazine*, September 18, 2005, p. 86.
3. Ibid., p. 83.
4. Martha Lagace, "How to Put Meaning Back into Leading," *Harvard Business School Working Knowledge,* January 10, 2005.
5. George Siemens, "Meaning-Making," September 2005 post on Connectivism Blog, www.connectivism.ca/blog/34.
6. Peggy Kreimer, "Medicare Drug Benefit a Study in Complexity," *Cincinnati Post,* October 29, 2005.
7. Michael Hiltzik, "Medicare Drug Plan Looks Like a Big Scam," *Latimes.com,* January 19, 2006.
8. From speech, "The Future of Marketing," by Jim Stengel, global marketing officer, The Proctor & Gamble Company, to the AAAA Media Conference, February 12, 2004.
9. Patricia Wolfe, *Brain Matters: Translating Research into Classroom Practice,* (Alexandria, Va.: Association for Supervision & Curriculum Development, July 2001).
10. Eric Jensen, *Teaching with the Brain in Mind* (Alexandria, Va.: Association for Supervision & Curriculum Development, April 1998), p. 92.
11. From transcript of *The Connection,* WBUR-FM, Boston, June 2, 2005.
12. See www.3aday.org/3aday/momscorner.
13. Constantine von Hoffman, "Inside the Box," *CMO Magazine,* September 2005, p. 27.
14. Geoffrey Colvin, "What's Love Got to Do with It?" *Fortune,* November 12, 2001, p. 60.
15. Jack Welch, *Winning* (New York: HarperCollins, 2005), p. 87
16. "Storytelling That Moves People: A Conversation with Screenwriting Coach Robert McKee," *Harvard Business Review,* June 2003.
17. Alex (Sandy) Pentland, "Socially Aware Computation and Communication," IEEE Computer Society, March 2005, p. 63.
18. From meeting in which author participated, October 2003.

19. Howard Gardner, *The Unschooled Mind: How Children Think & How Schools Should Teach* (New York: Basic Books, 1991), p. 111.

20. Quoted in "How I Make Decisions: Discovering Harry Potter," *Fortune,* June 27, 2005, p. 123.

Chapter 3. Have a fresh point of view (or several)

1. Raymond Yeh, *The Art of Business: In the Footsteps of Giants* (Olathe, Colo.: Zero Time Publishing, 2004).

2. Robert Hof, "Building an Idea Factory," *Business Week,* October 11, 2004, p. 200.

3. Betsy Morris, "Charles Schwab's Big Challenge," *Fortune,* May 30, 2005, p. 99.

4. Stephen Shankland, "Sun President: PCs Are So Yesterday," CNET News.com, September 23, 2005.

5. Jennifer Cattaui, "The World According to Sharp," Neiman Marcus "The Book" catalogue, April 2006.

6. Joe Lambert, *Digital Storytelling Cookbook and Traveling Companion* (Berkeley, Calif.: Digital Diner Press, May 2003), p. 10.

7. Kevin J. Clancy and Peter Krieg, *Counterintuitive Marketing: Achieve Great Results Using Uncommon Sense* (New York: The Free Press, 2000), pp. 109–110.

8. From the American Canadian Caribbean Cruise Line Web site, www .accl-smallships.com.

9. James Snyder, "Seven Tips for Writing a Great Campaign Speech," *Campaigns & Elections,* February 2000.

10. William Safire, *Safire's Political Dictionary* (New York: Ballantine Books, 1987).

11. Interview with author, March 2005.

12. Interview with author, January 2006.

13. David Kirkpatrick, "Still Feisty After All These Years," *Fortune,* October 31, 2005, p. 42.

14. Posted on Sun Microsystems Web site, www.sun.com.

15. Rob Walker, "Social Lubricant: How a Marketing Campaign Became the Catalyst for a Societal Debate," *The New York Times Magazine,* September 9, 2005, p. 23.

16. Dove Campaign for Real Beauty Web site, http://www.campaignfor realbeauty.com.

17. Interview with author, February 2006.

18. See www.womenandinfants.org.

19. Interview with author, February 2006.
20. Ibid.
21. Jim Collins, "Beware the Self-Promoting CEO," *The Wall Street Journal,* November 26, 2001, A18.
22. Stephanie Mehta, "Will Wall Street Ever Trust Time Warner?" *Fortune,* May 30, 2005, p. 83.

Chapter 4. Listen up: Seven ways to uncover talk-worthy ideas

1. Transcript of Rudy Giuliani commencement address to Middlebury College on May 22, 2005, from Middlebury College Web site.
2. David Kirkpatrick, "Throw It on the Wall and See If It Sticks," *Fortune,* December 12, 2005, p. 146.
3. Jaida N'Ha Sandra and Jon Spayde, *Salons: The Joy of Conversations* (Gabriola Island, B.C., Canada: New Society Publishers, 2001), p. 101.
4. Matt Bai, "The Framing Wars," *The New York Times Magazine,* July 17, 2005, p. 41.
5. Daniel Yankelovich, *The Magic of Dialogue: Transforming Conflict into Cooperation* (New York: Touchstone, 2001).
6. Jiddu Krishnamurti, *Talks and Dialogues* (New York: Avon Books, December 1986), p. 60.
7. Interview with author, February 2006.
8. Beagle Research Group, "Case Study: Communispace and Charles Schwab," January 2006.
9. Transcript from Alison Zelen's presentation to the American Marketing Association, September 27, 2005.
10. Alison Overholt, "New Leaders, New Agenda," *Fast Company,* May 2002, p. 52.
11. Aggregate customer consensus from SAP listening tour summary conducted by the author, May 2003.
12. Margaret Wheatley, Foreword to *The World Café: Shaping Our Futures Through Conversations That Matter* by Juanita Brown with David Isaacs and the World Café Community (San Francisco: Berrett-Koehler Publishers, 2005), p. xi.
13. "A Quick Reference Guide for Putting Conversations to Work," The World Café Community, 2002, www.worldcafe.com.
14. Jeffrey Blodgett, Ronald Granbois, and Rockney Walters, "The Effects of Perceived Justice on Complainants' Negative Word-of-Mouth Behavior and Repatronage Intentions," *The Journal of Retailing,* vol. 69. no. 4, Winter 1993, p. 399.

15. Bettina Cornwell and Len Coote, "Antecedents and Outcomes of Consumer Advocacy," University of Queensland Business School and Sam Friend, general manager, Wotif.com.
16. Michael Ende, *Momo,* translated by J. Maxell Brownjohn (New York: Random House, 1973).
17. Many thanks to creativity guru and award-winning advertising creative director Tom Monahan, author of *The Do It Yourself Lobotomy,* who taught me the value of 100 mph brainstorming more than fifteen years ago.
18. Gregg Levoy, *Callings: Finding and Following an Authentic Life* (New York: Harmony Books, 1997), p. 41.
19. George Lakoff and Mark Johnson, *Metaphors We Live By* (Chicago: University of Chicago Press, 1980), p. 3.
20. Author conversation with Chuck Dietsche, January 2006.
21. Suzy Wetlaufer, "Driving Change: An Interview with Ford Motor Company's Jacques Nasser," *Harvard Business Review,* March–April 1999, p. 87.
22. Joseph Nocera, "His Airline Didn't Skimp on the Cheese," *The New York Times,* January 7, 2006, p. B1.
23. "Letters to the Editor," *Harvard Business Review,* May 2005.
24. Yvon Chouinard, *Let My People Go Surfing: The Education of a Reluctant Businessman* (New York: Penguin Press, 2005).

Chapter 5. Nine themes that always get people talking

1. Interview with author, January 2006.
2. Yvon Chouinard, *Let My People Go Surfing: The Education of a Reluctant Businessman* (New York: Penguin Press, 2005).
3. Isabelle Chan, "Technology Can Help David Beat Goliath," Special SMB Report 2005, http://www.zdnetasia.com/smb/specialreports/2005/1.
4. Don Hay, "David vs. Goliath: An E-Mail Marketing Story," Hotel News Resource, www.hotelnewsresource.com, October 11, 2005.
5. Daniel Lyons, "Bang for the Buck," *Forbes,* November 25, 2002, p. 222.
6. Moon Ihlwan, "BMW, Mercedes—and Hyundai?" *Business Week,* December 5, 2005, p. 52.
7. Max Frankel, "Where There's Fear, There's News," *The New York Times Magazine,* June 29, 1997, p. 22.
8. National Academy of Sciences, "Above the Gathering Storm: Energizing and Employing America for a Brighter Economic Future," October 2005.

9. Timothy O'Brien, "Not Invented Here," *The New York Times,* November 13, 2005, www.nytimes.com.
10. Larry Summers, speech at National Bureau of Economic Research conference, January 2005. A transcript of the speech was posted on the Web site of the Office of the President of Harvard University, but has since been removed.
11. Ibid.
12. Kishore Mahbubani, *Can Asians Think?* 3rd ed. (Singapore: Times Editions, 2004).
13. Sin-Ming Shaw, "It's True. Asians Can't Think," *Time Asia,* May 31, 1999, www.timeasia.com.
14. Joshua Freed, "The Customer Is Always Right? Not Anymore," Associated Press Business Writer, *San Francisco Chronicle*, July 5, 2005, www.sfgate.com.
15. From transcript of Jim Skinner's keynote speech to the 2005 Business for Social Responsibility annual conference.
16. Ibid.
17. Robert Goizueta, "In His Own Words," *The Wall Street Journal,* October 20, 1997, p. 31.
18. Bruce Horovitz, "CEO Turns the Flame Up," *USA TODAY,* January 9, 2006, www.usatoday.com.
19. Steve Jobs, "Stay Hungry. Stay Foolish," *Fortune,* September 2, 2005, 31.
20. John Costello, "First Person Innovation: John Costello, Executive VP of Merchandising and Marketing, Home Depot," *CMO Magazine,* September 2005, p. 32.
21. James Clash and Robert Lenzer, "The $500 Billion Hedge Fund Folly," *Forbes,* August 6, 2001, www.forbes.com.
22. Randall Rothenberg, "The Dilemma of 'Star Branding,'" *Advertising Age,* February 27, 2006, www.adage.com.
23. Geraldine Fabrikant, "Talking Money with Sarah Jessica Parker: From a Start on Welfare to Riches in the City," *The New York Times,* July 30, 2000, section 3, p. 1.

Chapter 6. Straight talk: Talk like you talk, talk like you mean it, talk in these ten new ways

1. Thanks to Howie Jacobson from whom I first heard the term *Doglish.* "My Dog No Longer Thinks I'm a Moron," *HowieConnect* newsletter, October 17, 2003.
2. Patricia McConnell, *The Other End of the Leash* (New York: Ballantine Books, 2003).

3. Suzy Wetlaufer, "Driving Change: An Interview with Ford Motor Company's Jacques Nasser," *Harvard Business Review,* March–April 1999, p. 84.

4. "Follow These Leaders," *Fortune* special section, December 12, 2005.

5. Bronwyn Fryer, "Storytelling That Moves People: A Conversation with Screenwriting Coach Robert McKee," *Harvard Business Review,* June 2003, p. 7.

6. Bob Wyss, "Keeping the First Person Above Water," December 6, 2000, www.projo.com/words.

7. Sean Silverthorne, "Book Report: 'More Space: Nine Antidotes to Complacency,'" *Harvard Business School Working Knowledge,* November 21, 2005, www.hbswk.edu.

8. Joe Lambert, *Digital Storytelling Cookbook and Traveling Companion* (Berkeley, Calif.: Digital Diner Press, 2003), p. 3.

9. "Bringing Company Values to Life," *CMO Magazine,* September 2005, p. 52.

10. Kate Bonamici, "The Shoe In: How CEO Jeffrey Schwartz Keeps Timberland Firmly Planted on Our List," *Fortune,* January 23, 2006, www.cnnmoney.com.

11. Jack Welch, *Winning* (New York: HarperCollins, 2005), p. 25.

12. Mario Cuomo, "The Lost Oration," *Esquire,* February 2002, p. 90.

13. Jeff Foxworthy interview transcript, "Paul Harris Show," www.harrisonline.com, May 30, 1996.

Chapter 7. Shift to a conversational marketing mind-set

1. 2005 Yankelovich Marketing Receptivity Study.

2. Catharine Taylor, "Psst! How Do You Measure Buzz?" *ADWEEK,* October 24, 2005, p. 26.

3. Margaret Singer comment on "Thy Will Be Done," a documentary produced in 1980 by WCCO-TV, Minneapolis.

4. Preface by Eric Utne to *Salons: The Joy of Conversations,* by Jaida N'Ha Sandra and John Spayde (Gabriola Island, B.C., Canada: New Society of Publishers, 2001), p. vi.

5. Deborah Tannen, *You Just Don't Understand* (New York: Ballantine Books, 1991), p. 77.

6. Interview with author, January 2006.

7. Business Innovation Factory's BIF-1 Conference, Providence, R.I., October 2005.

8. Interview with author, February 2006.

9. Interview with author, January 2006.

10. Alan Stewart, "The Conversing Company: Its Culture, Power and Potential," presented at the First World Conference for Systematic Management, Vienna, May 2001, www.theworldcafe.com/conversing company.pdf.

Chapter 8. Building a "talk" culture

1. Peter Drucker, *On the Profession of Management* (Boston: Harvard Business School Press, 1998), p. 95.
2. Tomi T. Ahonen and Alan Moore, *Communities Dominate Brands: Business and Marketing Challenges for the 21st Century* (London: Futurtext, 2005), p. 229.
3. John Deigthon, "How Snapple Got Its Juice Back," *Harvard Business Review*, January 2002, p. 52.
4. Landon Thomas Jr., "When C.E.O.s Are Entangled in Their Own Web of Words," *The New York Times*, November 9, 2005, p. C2.
5. Paul Argenti, *Corporate Communication* (New York: Irwin/McGraw Hill, 1998), p. 52.
6. Gary Hamel, *Leading the Revolution* (Boston: Harvard Business School Press, 2002), p. 152.

Chapter 9. Be more interesting—conversations, passion, and an honest point of view

1. Bryan Rourke, "RISD Grad the Soul Proprietor of the Latest Oddity on eBay," *The Providence Journal*, March 4, 2006, p. A3.
2. Raymond Hernandez, "On Podium, Some Say, Mrs. Clinton Is No Mr. Clinton," *The New York Times*, February 3, 2006, www.nytimes.com.
3. Ibid.
4. From Jim Skinner's keynote speech to the 2005 Business for Social Responsibility Conference.
5. "McDonald's Not Lovin' 'McJob' Dictionary Definition," Associated Press, November 10, 2003.
6. From Jim Skinner's keynote speech to the 2005 Business for Social Responsibility Conference.
7. From David Whyte's CD "Life at the Frontier: Leadership Through Courageous Conversation," www.davidwhyte.com.

Index